WOMEN'S WAYS

WALKS BY SEVEN WOMEN FROM SHEFFIELD

SUE BEARDON

Identity Books

Published by Identity Books
and distributed by:
Mayfield Books & Gifts
9 Orgreave Close, Handsworth, Sheffield S13 9NP
Phone: 0800 834920 Email: sales@mayfield-books.co.uk

ISBN 978 1 902674 14 8

British Library Cataloguing in Publication Data.
A catalogue record for this book is available from the British Library.

Edited by Sue Beardon
Proofreading by Mike Reid
Design, typesetting and maps by Dick Richardson
Drawings by Jenny Fortune

Dedicated to the memory of
Rachel Heatley and Jos Kingston

Some of the money from this project will be donated to Medical
Aid for Palestinians and the Palestine Women's Scholarship
Fund.

Printed and bound in England by: Kingsbury Press, Doncaster

Contents

INTRODUCTION

Seven of us have put this book together and each section of the book contains walks chosen and led by one of us. We hope we will convey our enthusiasm for walking in this book and that it will inspire readers, female or male, to try some new walks. Walking is something we love and we have done for years and nothing short of physical incapacity will stop us. We walk for a host of reasons. There's contact with nature and with the elements. There's adventure as well as awareness of changing seasons and the natural environment we live in. We also enjoy the companionship and the deepening of friendship through conversations or through experiences shared. We sometimes walk just to enjoy solitude and stillness in nature.

We are aware of a long tradition of women walkers that we inherit. We came across this piece in the Sheffield Clarion Ramblers Handbook, from fifty years ago:

Sunday, November 27th, 1960.
Ladies ONLY. Rough ramble.
    'Bus: 8-30 a.m. Pond St. No. 48. Manchester to Woodhead. Return from Derwent. Fare. 4/-.
    Only ladies accustomed to rough moorland walking should attend. Boots essential.
Leader: Miss M. R. Shaw.

Sheffield Clarion Ramblers Handbook 160

The walks in this book are varied in length, difficulty and terrain. You can choose to walk Jill's Slice of Sheffield, an easy walk perfectly possible with a pushchair. Jenny and Cathy have contributed walks which can be strung together as long distance epics. Sue has offered an off-piste romp over Pike Low and a linear walk out to Hathersage across little known Access Land, requiring use of public transport. Debby and Heather both offer walks which are redolent of memories

All ready to set off from the General Cemetery in Sheffield
Michael Reid

for them of dear friends and extraordinary events. Sally is well known for her interest in walks with a local history element, and offers one here, along with poetry – her own and others'.

Most of these walks can be followed by using the notes and drawings and referring to the relevant Ordnance Survey maps. Mostly the walks are on the White Peak and Dark Peak Ordnance Survey maps, and some spread onto the Sheffield map in the same series. A section on navigation in this book explains some basic principles of using a map and compass. Whatever you do – happy walking!

5

SUE

Sue Beardon

Loves walking the hills,
singing the blues
and changing
the world, and then
during the week…

When I was a child my father would tell me about legendary mountain climbers, who seemed to me to be remote, exotic figures, often aristocratic and of course always men. My school told me about Sir Edmund Hillary, but I never heard of the many women who climbed in the Alps. Certainly no woman in my family would ever have thought of such a thing.

I rediscovered the joy of walking in my 30s. I was taken to Ingleton in the Three Peaks area of the Yorkshire Dales. I remember seeing the profile of Ingleborough Hill as we made our way from Lancaster through to Bentham. It looked somewhat like a tiered wedding cake with the whitish limestone like royal icing.

Through my walking club I learned about navigation and safety in the hills and began to enjoy solitary walks, navigating my way around wild terrain away from well known footpaths. I walked longer and longer distances, enjoying the challenge and the pulsing of the blood.

The opportunities for women to be whatever they want are legion now. Although I am still often caught short by comments I receive on the hills. Once a man walked past a group of us, all women, as we walked along Froggatt Edge. He said, "I've just seen another group of all ladies ahead of you", as if this were a strange and exotic thing. Somehow I found the wit to say straight back, "Our husbands sometimes let us out when they don't need us to cook dinner". His wife laughed. "You asked for that" she said.

I like walking on my own. I love the solitude. But I also love to walk with my precious friends, especially my women friends. There are so many different ways of walking and enjoying landscape, from being utterly attentive to what is before one's eyes, to having a beautiful backdrop to a sociable day with friends, to setting oneself challenges, to allowing the mind to take its course as one enjoys the freedom of the outdoors. Any of these are fine with me, and I have indulged in all of them.

The first walk I have chosen, from Langsett to Bolsterstone, Heather and I undertook on a beautiful day during summer. Because we were doing it on a Saturday, there was no direct bus to Langsett and we decided our best bet was to take the train to Barnsley and then bus from there. Unfortunately we chose the day of Penistone Summer Show and traffic was snarled up for miles around, making our journey rather longer than we had anticipated.

We both enjoy these moorland walks, far from the crowds that flock to Peak District honey pots. Even though the popular Langsett Reservoir is very close, out on Pike Low, not a soul is to be seen. We reflected on the fact that although the moor was peaceful now, it has frequently been a place of preparation for war, as well as for the shooting of grouse.

But by the time we had arrived at the bus stop near Bolsterstone we felt thoroughly imbued with a sense of peace. It was unfortunate therefore that we arrived into the Hillsborough area to coincide with football crowds leaving the ground. Our tram was soon taken over by a heaving, rowdy crowd, banging on windows and raucously chanting. We remarked that it was fortunate that hill walkers prefer not to gather in large tribes and chant loudly and disparagingly about rivals. We laughed as we imagined how that might have sounded on top of Pike Low.

My second walk is one I have loved for a long time and which thanks to the CROW Act is no longer a trespass. It takes you from Lodge Moor, on the edge of Sheffield, across to Stanage Edge over empty moorland and thence to Hathersage.

Finally I describe a walk very close to Sheffield, an urban centre with a vast industrial heritage but with green fingers of valleys snaking into it from the surrounding countryside. This walk is a favourite of mine, not because it is the prettiest, wildest or most fascinating. It gives me the same feeling that going to the cinema on a mid-week afternoon does. I just feel like I am getting something extra, pleasure at a time or in a place that I am not supposed to be having.

Heather, Jenny and I set off one wintry Saturday at the beginning of January to take

Sue with her grandchildren at Stanage
Jenny Fortune

Supertram from outside the Cathedral in Sheffield. As we emerged from the tram at Malin Bridge sleety, cold moisture was falling in a most unpromising way. Dressed for the cold and wet we trudged on, and we were to be rewarded, as the sleet turned to large fluffy flakes of snow falling in woodland. Part of our walk took us above Loxley Cemetery as we traversed Acorn Hill. This was significant for us because it was exactly 10 years ago that a dear friend of ours had been killed in a climbing accident and buried in the woodland burial ground there. So three became four for a while, as we carried her memory with us.

We decided to end our walk in Hillsborough, near the football ground, where the marvellous Cupola Gallery can be found. Crowds were roaring at Hillsborough stadium, where a match was in progress. But we enjoyed the tranquillity of the gallery where there was an extremely appropriate exhibition around the theme of "Ice".

Lady Cross, above Salter's Brook, looking West
Jenny Patient

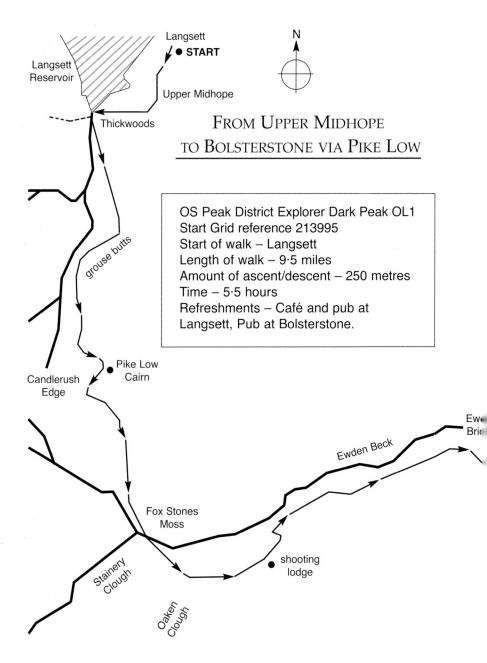

From Upper Midhope
to Bolsterstone via Pike Low

OS Peak District Explorer Dark Peak OL1
Start Grid reference 213995
Start of walk – Langsett
Length of walk – 9·5 miles
Amount of ascent/descent – 250 metres
Time – 5·5 hours
Refreshments – Café and pub at
Langsett, Pub at Bolsterstone.

Take the bus to Langsett and back from Bolsterstone. Buses run from Sheffield to Langsett on Sundays and from Bolsterstone take the tram link to Middlewood and then the tram back to Sheffield.

● The walk starts from a small parking spot at GR 213995, which is reached from Langsett by walking across the dam, south down a track through Upper Midhope and onto a small road. Turn right here and through a gate onto Thickwoods Lane, through woods. After crossing Thickwoods Brook a path goes up to the left and meets a track above a farm.

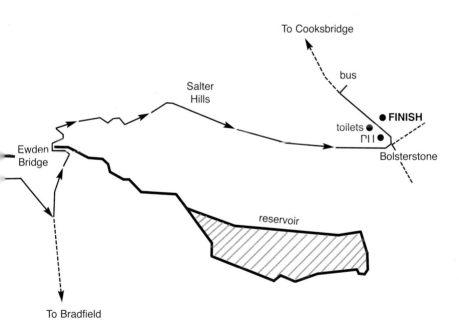

Langsett Bank Woods is an example of how woodland can be managed to serve a number of different purposes. Planted in the 1920s by Sheffield Corporation Waterworks, the trees helped to stabilise the steep reservoir bank. The roots hold the soil of the bank and stop it from being washed into the reservoir. Langsett Bank Woods are managed for the preservation of water quality, as an environmental area for encouraging wildlife and for felling to produce wood for fences and pulp for paper.

- Turn right onto the track which soon splits into three. Take the left hand track up onto Range Moor and keep south over a little rise. Once over the rise slightly to your right is a disused target. From here a line of grouse butts is easily followed along a stream. A little higher the rocky slope up onto Pike Low is seen to your left. You can take a direct line up to the cairn on top at any point.

- Find the summit cairn and from here go south onto Candlerush Edge and follow the path with guide posts to the left. When you are almost at the last post a large stream gully goes down to the right. Follow this direction as best you can until you see Spring Gutter valley down ahead. Keep going south towards it until arriving above the stream near Fox Stones Moss.

- Keep left above the stream until you catch up with an indistinct path, which soon goes down through bracken to the stream. Follow this path past the lovely little waterfall over large mossy blocks. The last part of the path is not always obvious, but stays close to the stream all the way to the confluence with Stainery Clough. Flat rocks around this area will often have dippers on them and it's a gorgeous place for a solitary stop. I've never seen anyone here.

- There's no easy way from here. You need to go south up the opposite bank, the best place being about 10 metres or so up Stainery Clough, through birch trees. When you arrive on less steep ground you will see the Shooting Lodge you are heading for next.

Climb a bit higher before going towards it and keep your eyes open for a path, sheep track really, snaking through the bilberry and heather to Oaken Clough. You have to cross this. A path goes down by a fallen tree and across a couple of small streams to reach the bottom of the clough and climbs the other side. Keep going east towards the shooting lodge – if you're lucky you'll stay on the path, but it's easily lost.

Salt was taken across the Pennines from Cheshire to Yorkshire, to be used in a variety of processes, from soap making to curing meat. Many of the place names testify to this trade, such as Salter Hills and Salts Spring.

- Once at the lodge go left on a really good wide track. Follow this through a lovely valley with rhododendrons until reaching the road from Bradfield to Stocksbridge. There are a number of ways to go from here to Bolsterstone. We turned left onto the road and followed it down over Ewden Beck and up the other side, to find a path on the right that goes through fields of cows and woodland up to Salter Hills. The path crosses a field, and then goes through a gate into a field that usually has cows in it. It skirts a small copse, often very muddy and crosses a small stream. Then keep uphill of the hedge dividing the two fields towards a copse and another stream. There is a gap through the trees and you cross the stream and keep going through woodland. Emerging from woods the path climbs and eventually arrives at a lane where you turn right. From here you can detour up the hill to the trig point which lies just above the lane. It is a straightforward walk along the lane, which then becomes a metalled road, through to Bolsterstone.

- After a well earned rest at the pub, go left out of the pub towards Stocksbridge and take the first turning right. There is a bus stop just a few yards along the first street on the left where you can catch the very frequent Supertram Link to Middlewood for trams and buses to the city centre. Other less frequent buses do go from Bolsterstone village itself.

During the Second World War, following the air raids on Sheffield, the authorities decided to create a mock village on the moors. The purpose was that when enemy aircraft were expected, a unit from the Defence Regiment would go onto the moors and light powder charges to make the enemy think that they were bombing a large area. This proved to be unsuccessful on two counts, one being that the Germans had far better surveillance and navigation aids than the British thought, and secondly the regiment could not find its way in the dark. It was decided that local farmers should act as guides and lead the regiment to the spot.

A rocky outcrop above the Derwent Valley
Jenny Patient

14

Woodland view in winter
Jill Angood

15

The Derwent Valley
Jenny Patient

LODGE MOOR TO HATHERSAGE

OS Sheffield and Barnsley Explorer 278 Start Grid reference 284863
Start of walk – Lodge Moor
Length of walk – 8·5 miles
Ascent – 220 metres
Time – 4·5 hours
Refreshments – pubs and cafés at Hathersage

You take the number 51 bus to the end of its journey at Lodge Moor hospital. From there continue a short way along the main road, crossing over to take the first footpath to the right. After about 250 metres and just after a left hand bend, the path forks and you take the right fork that gradually drops down through trees to Rivelin Reservoirs.

• The track follows the reservoir for a short while, and then begins to rise through woods. The track swings round to the right, crossing Reddicar Clough. On the far side of the clough there is a narrow path that rises steeply to meet the main path across Head Stone Bank. Turn left onto this path and follow the bank to a cross roads with way marks.

• Turn left here, following a wall uphill to meet the conduit. Cross the stile on the right onto the path that follows the conduit. This used to be a trespass until the CROW Act, but now can be walked with out fear of contradiction. The path soon arrives at a delightful spot – a small reservoir with a little disused hut. Go round to the left keeping on a small path just above the reservoir that drops down in a short while to the stream. This is a boggy place and the stream can be swollen in wet weather. But if you keep the path on the other side in your sights there is a narrow place very nearby, which you can cross using a couple of stepping stones and clumps of grass. This is at a point around GR 247862.

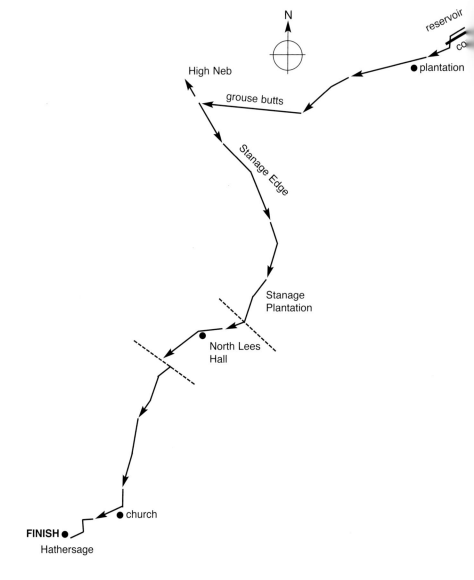

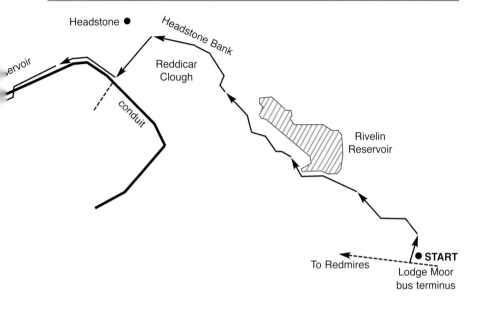

- Take the path on the other side going uphill towards a small plantation. You are heading for the right hand edge of it, the northern tip. Cross the plantation and walk south-west uphill, keeping close to a wall. Keep the wall on your right all the way across this section until reaching the highest point at 433m. You will see a clear path crossing the moor ahead along a line of grouse butts. Follow this west across the always boggy moor to a small shelter close to the edge of Stanage. A few more steps bring you to the edge and glorious views.

- Turn left and keeping to the edge for about a mile, find the path that goes down over rocks to meet and cross Stanage Plantation. Eventually the path reaches the road near a small building with public conveniences. The path to its left has a sign to Hathersage and Bamford. Follow this down, through a small gate, and to North Lees Hall. Take the drive down from the house to the road. Turn left here and look for the first footpath on the right which takes you past Cow Close. The way marks take you above and behind the house and farmyard. Follow the route across fields just above the valley bottom, going south. Cross a stile onto a very muddy path that soon descends slightly into the next field and crosses it towards the church.

Those of you, like me, who as little girls thrilled to the romantic story of Jane Eyre, will be pleased to know that North Lees Hall is thought to be the model for Rochester's mansion, with its mad wife in the west wing and its tragic end in a fire in which Rochester goes blind. Stirring stuff.

- There are wooden steps after crossing a small stream that lead up to the Church. It is well worth looking in at the churchyard to see Little John's grave. From the graveyard a path goes downhill to the right of a high wall, which after about 350 metres reaches a wide track. Turn left here to arrive in Hathersage, with cafes, shops, and buses and trains to Sheffield and other places. The bus stop is out side the Post Office. For the station go on the path on the opposite side of the main road, that goes through a church and car park to the swimming pool. Turn right and then left along the B6001 Grindleford Road and the station is on the left up a small road with modern buildings at the end.

Supertram walk from Malin Bridge to Hillsborough

OS Sheffield and Barnsley Explorer 278 Start Grid reference 328894
Start of walk – Malin Bridge
Length of walk – 7 miles
Ascent/descent – 200 metres
Time – 3·5 hours
Refreshments – Rheingold Garden Centre, Cupola Gallery, Hillsborough

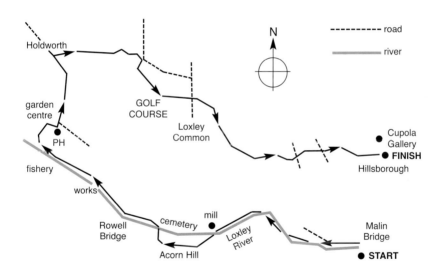

- From Malin Bridge tram stop walk westwards along the road to the junction and cross onto Loxley Road. A short way along this road there is a track going off to the left that takes the right bank of the stream. Follow this all the way until reaching the old Rolling Mill. It is a fascinating area of ancient trees, mill ponds and derelict industrial buildings. At the Mill go across the footbridge and at a small interpretation panel take the footpath going right angling gently uphill. Keep on this path across the side of Acorn Hill.

- Soon you have a choice of paths, either crossing the river again by another footbridge and along the track past a small reservoir to the road at Rowell Bridge, or staying on the same side and down past more ruined buildings and crossing the river slightly further up. In either case you end up at Rowell Bridge and cross the road, continuing into more woodland and staying on the right bank of the river.

- The path soon takes you out onto a wide track leading through more old industrial buildings. Keep through the buildings, taking a path to the right of them and eventually to the fishery. Keep on the path to the right of the fishing pond and continue on to Stacey Bank, with the large dam of Damflask reservoir ahead and a large walled reservoir to your left. Turn right up the lane onto the main road at a pub. Turn right here and take the first road on the left. Shortly the entrance to the garden centre can be seen, and the café visited if required.

- Go steeply up the road to Holdworth and take the first path on the right, after the road has bent round to the left and before farm buildings. The path cuts diagonally across the hillside in an easterly direction, and then into woodland past a lovely little wooden dwelling. Keep following the path as it comes out of the woodland and along a wall underneath huge farm buildings. As that path runs out there is a stile over the wall to the left and a short uphill stretch to meet the farm track. Turn right onto this.

- At the corner junction with Stubbing Lane take a gate to the right going downhill. At a junction of paths swing round to the left, following the way marks through the golf course. When you reach the road continue straight over onto a track. You are now entering the area of Loxley and Wadsley Commons. There is a plethora of paths here and all of them are pleasant and will eventually lead you down into Wadsley village. The most direct route to a tram stop here is to stay to the north on paths across Wadsley Common, down to the car park. Here turn left, then sharp right, then down the first turning on the left to arrive at Middlewood tram stop and park and ride.

- On our walk we chose to drop down the second path to the right about 400 metres from the road. This way you can visit the trig point on Loxley Edge and then drop down to Loxley House, down hill through residential areas of Hillsborough to the park and Leppings Lane tram stop. This has the advantage of allowing a visit to the Cupola Gallery, which almost always has exhibitions of note and interest, and the kind assistant will most likely offer you tea and coffee. If there is a football match on, do finish your walk and take the tram before it finishes, otherwise you can get caught up with the immense and noisy football crowd (see my Pike Low walk!), which is not to everyone's taste.

Debby

Debby Pickvance

I have lived on the west side of Sheffield for over thirty years and love the place especially because it is so close to wonderful countryside

The enjoyment I find in walking has much to do with what I absorbed of my parents' shared love of nature and walking – though I doubt they would have thought the girl who lagged behind her three older brothers and grumbled whenever there was a hill to climb would make much of a walker. My own children have been through much the same transformation and perhaps my grandchildren will too, as each generation discovers in its own way what its elders already know. Without planning it this way I realize these three walks reflect a birth, a death and the pleasure of living (and walking).

My first walk, a circular walk through Cressbrookdale, Millersdale and Tideswelldale, is lovely any time of year but best of all in the early summer when the lime-loving flowers are in bloom – orchids, rock rose, cranesbill and many more. But I have chosen it because it was the scene of a memorable event. One day walking along a track beside the narrow strip fields at Litton, Heather and I saw a cow lying alone in a field in a strange position. As we drew closer we realised the cow was in labour. After pausing to wonder whether to let nature take its course we decided to try and let the farmer know and headed for a farmhouse nearby. The woman there gestured us to turn back to the public footpath when she saw us approach, but she was glad we had ignored her when she heard the news and she went to phone the farmer straightaway.

We then went back and watched the cow, which was by now bellowing and sweating with the effort of giving birth. But we were not the only ones who had noticed something out of the ordinary was happening. In the next field three cows came up to the wall, looked over and began mooing loudly, as if to say, 'We've all been there, love... You can do it... One more push...' Fanciful anthropomorphising perhaps, but it is hard not to think these were encouraging sounds for the labouring cow.

After what felt like ages the calf was born, but, still wrapped in its cowl, it lay on the ground showing little sign of life. It was a great relief to us when a tractor hove into view along the track. The farmer jumped out, leapt nimbly over the stone wall into the field, unceremoniously picked the calf up by its back legs, and swung it against the ground to wipe the mucus from its mouth and nose. A few uneven lurching breaths followed. The farmer stood back to let the cow take over, her teats dripping with milk by this time. We all watched, moved and relieved, as she nudged and nuzzled her calf into life.

My second walk, from Hathersage to Carr Head Rocks, is in memory of Jos Kingston, a good friend who died of cancer in 2007. She was known to many women in Sheffield as a feminist, campaigner and founding member of the Sheffield Women's Printing Co-op. She was also a keen walker and after she moved to Hathersage in 2000 it was a great pleasure to visit her and walk with her on some of the numerous footpaths she knew so well. Walks invariably started and finished with cups of tea at her home and interesting conversation was guaranteed. After she became ill, walking became one of the key ways she looked after her health and she impressed medical staff and others with her stamina. This walk had a particular significance for her – it was one she loved to do and to take her friends on, even though it starts with a steady ascent of 250 metres, which is not easy when lung function is weakening. There were points on it which she savoured (noted below) and the view from Carr Head Rocks was a great reward for reaching her goal. It felt a privilege to walk with her in the last couple of years of her life, when she talked candidly of her thoughts about living and dying. A flavour of these and much more can be found on her website www.joskingston.org (a website address which has the unusual distinction of being recorded on her gravestone in Hathersage burial ground). This walk is part of a longer one which some of her friends and family walk annually around the time of her birthday, continuing to raise money through sponsorship for her chosen charity, Medical Aid for Palestinians.

The last walk, around Bradfield, is one of contrasts – within a few hours it passes through woods and valleys, beside water, along an edge and over moorland, and offers fine views towards Derwent Edge and the peat moorland of the Dark Peak. The countryside around Bradfield is quieter than many areas further south in the Peak District – this helps to make the walk all the more refreshing and relaxing. Rocher Edge is a fraction the length of its popular southern neighbours at Stanage or Froggatt, yet it is a terrific vantage point. In the right season you can hear curlews and sky-larks on the high ground, gaze at jackdaws flying above the rocks on the Edge or watch woodland birds pecking from the birdfeeders in Windy Bank Wood.

Bradfield has its own delights – a beautifully situated church, a churchyard grazed by sheep, a miniature topiary hedge in front of a house nearby, ducks and swans on the river by the bridge, and a post office – still open – which doubles as a cafe. Over the years I have caught snatches of local carols sung in the Old Horns Inn on December Sundays, enjoyed a cool drink in the sunny garden of the Plough at the end of a long hot day or sat beside the cricket pitch after calling at the ice-cream van. The day I did this walk with Sue and Jill we plodded through deep snow and passed frozen ponds.

This walk, or some variant of it, is where I find myself heading again and again, whether going out by arrangement with friends or just wanting some fresh air on a Sunday afternoon before facing another contrast – the urban landscape of my work – the following day.

Dales of the White Peak

OS Peak District Explorer White Peak OL4.
Start Grid reference 752165
Start point – Wardlow or Litton
Length – 6 miles
Ascent – 300 metres
Time – 3·5 hours
Refreshments – Pub and Post Office at Litton

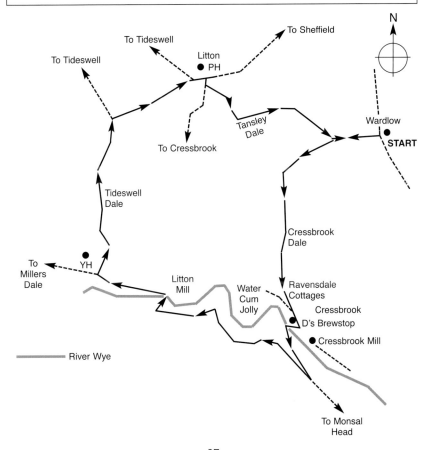

The advantage of starting the walk in Wardlow is that you start high. Of course, if you are returning to the same point you will need to regain that height at the end of the walk. The advantage of starting at Litton is that buses stop there and there are good opportunities for refreshments if you end the walk there. There are many variations on this walk. The route described is a favourite that gives some lovely airy views but without too many scary moments. Some of the paths can be quite precipitous, but we avoid those in this version.

- From Wardlow take the path that leaves the B6465 Wardlow to Ashford road just south of the pub. The path goes west to the edge of Cressbrook Dale and then drops down into the dale. You could do the walk either way, but to do the route clockwise, take the path to the left and follow it down Cressbrook Dale to Ravensdale Cottages. Follow the road up from the cottages to the road and continue downhill into the bottom end of Cressbrook and Cressbrook Mill. Turn right just before the mill and pass D's Brewstop.

- From here cross the stream at the weir and go up the limestone steps the other side to get onto the Monsal Trail. Follow the trail towards Monsal Head for a short while. Take the first good path you see on the right, which doubles back up the hill. If you have reached the old railway path you have gone too far.

- Follow the path along the edge for about one and a half kilometres. You will come to some old adits, entrances to old mine workings which now just look like caves. At the cave take the path leading downhill which arrives at the old railway as it would have disappeared into a tunnel. Continue along the track until the path on the right that goes down to cross the river and into the hamlet of Litton Mill. By the tunnel entrance there is a board that tells you about the mill and the heartless mill owner, who lived in what is now Ravenstor Youth Hostel. The mill is now apartments.

- At the hamlet turn left and continue for about half a kilometre until the path goes off right to go up Tideswell Dale. At the end of this delightful dale you reach a car park, and follow a path that goes parallel to the road until it reaches the junction with the right turn to Litton. Go along the road into the village of Litton, which is definitely worth a visit. The Red Lion pub is pleasant and the village store and post office was taken over by local people when it was threatened with closure and is run as a co-operative.

- If you are ending the walk here buses go back to Sheffield. If you are continuing to Wardlow, go through the village, take the road to the right to Cressbrook and when the road turns right, take the track which goes off to the left. Walk along this track passing several narrow fields (one of which was where the calf was born) and then take the waymarked path over a stile into a field that drops down into Tansley Dale. Follow this path until it meets up with the main path you started on that goes down to Cressbrook. Go right and up hill to regain your outward path back to Wardlow.

Carr Head Rocks

CARR HEAD ROCKS

OS Peak District Explorer Dark Peak OL1.
Start Grid reference 233816
Start of walk – Hathersage
Length of walk – 2·5 miles
Amount of ascent/descent – 200 metres
Time – 1·5 hours
Refreshments – Cafés and pubs in Hathersage

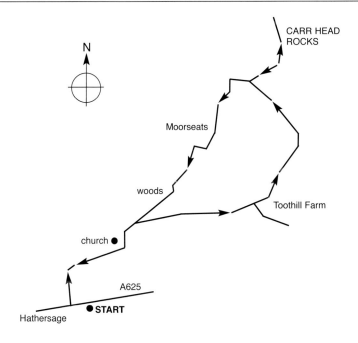

From the main street take Baulk Lane, the track which goes beside the Hathersage Inn. Walk along this track until you come to a path on the right hand side which goes up hill beside a wall to the church. Follow this path up to the churchyard. Jos's grave is in the Hathersage burial

31

ground on the right of the path. The churchyard has several ancient yew trees which Jos liked to stop at – see 'Yew, me, Highlow and Hathersage' on her web-site for more about this.

- Go out of the churchyard through the lych-gate and turn left on to a lane. Go over a stile and follow a path which forks and ascends to the right hand side. Look for a gate on the right hand side, go through this and turn left on to a tarmacked lane. Follow this lane up the hill. You will walk past a mature beech tree with huge spreading roots on the left hand side of this lane where Jos loved to look at the view across to Highlow.

- Take a path on the right just before a cattle grid and continue up the hill. Before you reach Toothill farm buildings follow the path left into the next field and immediately right, continuing to climb until the path reaches the top of the next field and you go through a gate and turn left on to another path. This path reaches a track where you turn left. Continue on this track until you come to a small gate on the right hand side signed access land. Go through this gate and climb up the path until you reach Carr Head rocks on your left hand side. The views from Carr Head rocks are magnificent – up Hope Valley, across to Kinder Scout, with Stanage Edge as a sort of elongated amphitheatre behind you. You can look down to the valley between Hathersage and North Lees where Jos achieved a local victory by persuading the new owner of Brookfield Manor to allow public use of his drive.

- To return to Hathersage retrace your steps to the track, turn right on to it and follow it down past Kimber Court Farm and Moorseats. Take a sharp right (partially obscured by a hedge) and follow a path, keeping the field containing a helipad on your left. Turn left just before reaching a gate, and go down a path through lovely woodland. Follow this path out of Moorseats wood through a wooden doorway, across two fields and back to the church, and then retrace your steps to Hathersage.

View of Highlow from the churchyard, Hathersage

AROUND BRADFIELD

OS Peak District Explorer Dark Peak OL1
Start Grid reference 268924
Start point – High Bradfield
Length – 6 miles
Ascent – 250 metres
Time – 4 hours
Refreshments – Postcard Café and the Plough Inn at Low Bradfield, Horns Inn, High Bradfield

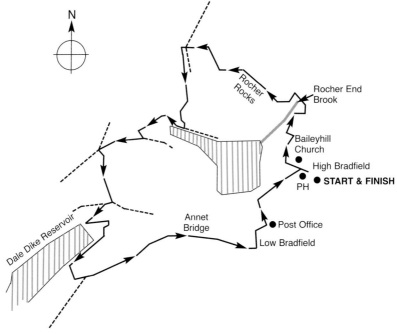

● From High Bradfield go into the churchyard and onto the path that stays high, going underneath the mound of the ancient mott and bailey site and into mixed woodland. After about 400 metres from here the path turns sharply left down hill. Where it meets a track turn right going up the right hand bank of a stream. This track bends right to go up to the road, but before a gate it is possible to divert off to the left, walk across two fields, turn left on to a track around the head of Rocher End Brook and then fork right onto a narrow access path onto the top of Rocher Rocks. Keep on the edge for about one kilometre and look out for a path just past a bench that heads down steeply to the left and meets a stile near the farm buildings of Rocher Head. Turn right here along the muddy track to reach the road.

Notice on church gate at High Bradfield
Debby Pickvance

- Cross the road and over the stile into the next field. Not far into this field look out for a stile in the wall on the left that takes you onto another road. Cross this road and over the stile opposite. Follow this path, soon crossing another stile, and following a wall along the top of an edge. The path then turns right to drop steeply down Agden Side to the edge of Agden reservoir. Turn right to the far end of the reservoir, then follow the path round to the left to arrive at a junction of paths. Take the one straight ahead that goes uphill following Emlin Dike and eventually to the road. Turn right uphill on the road, past Wilkin Hall to the junction with a more main road at the top.

- Turn left and immediately take the first footpath left that drops down to Dale Road. Turn right and then climb over a stile on to a track on the left. Soon after joining this track you will see a small memorial on the left to victims of the Great Sheffield Flood in 1864, in which the dam of the Dale Dike Reservoir burst and the valley was flooded. The memorial is in the position of one end of the old dam. The track bears left at a fork and winds down through woods to reach Dale Dike just after it emerges from Dale Dike reservoir. Cross the dike on a footbridge, climbing up steps the other side and continue along the dike to reach the edge of the reservoir. After a few hundred metres there is a seat with a stile behind it. After a stop here, cross the stile into the wood and go uphill through the wood to a track which goes left to reach the road.

- Turn left onto the road and continue along it for a little more than one kilometre. Just before Annet Bridge take the footpath on the right that follows just above Dale Dike to reach Mill Lee Road on the outskirts of Low Bradfield. Go left past an old chapel and then right across the bridge into the village. The Post Office is on the right where the road starts to rise up to High Bradfield. It has a lovely café and delicious soup in winter, as well as a book exchange.

- After a well earned stop at the café it is an easy although uphill stroll back to High Bradfield, taking the path behind the cricket field, past the new village hall and along a small stream. Steps go steeply up to the right onto a path that continues, crossing a road and back up towards the Church at High Bradfield.

If you are using buses you could end the walk at Low Bradfield and take the bus back from there. Buses to and from Bradfield go from Hillsborough Interchange, reached by tram from Sheffield Centre.

JILL

Jill Angood

Usually to be found happily esconced at the back of any walking group, with the excuse that my Fenland legs have not yet evolved for going uphill fast.

I first moved to Sheffield in the mid 1970s and have always loved the way you can see out of the city to the hills, and get that glimpse of green from the centre of town. So my first walk, Slice of Sheffield, epitomises the ease with which you can reach the countryside from the city just by using your feet ...and of course, you can always get a bus back if you (or your smaller companions) run out of energy for the return journey. It's not only a single round walk, but also a necklace of smaller round walks to suit different occasions.

As a single walk, it takes me almost all the way from the back door of my home in inner city Sheffield straight out to the open countryside of the Peak District through some beautiful parks and urban landscapes. Or I can choose to break it down into any one of several self contained loops, giving me choices about how far to go and how long I have to enjoy the outside. I can also use buses to join the walk at either end, or to leave it in the middle. I have walked most of it with a push chair, some with a child in a back pack, and on one occasion tackled it with a broken arm.

At any time of year there are precious gifts along the way – I have enjoyed glimpses of kingfishers on the Porter Brook as well as relishing the brilliance of autumn colour or trees iced with frost as you climb up to Ringinglow. It's great to see the joy in a child's face as they try out their new bike in Endcliffe Park and to stand amazed at tropical colours and scents in the Botanical Gardens.

The walk is full of differing landscapes. There are the ones I see *now*, on *this* walk in *this* season with *this* person, but also there is the way these landscapes are experienced through a filter of remembered walks in other seasons with other people.

In particular I get glimpses of my own past when I spent more time with young children. Women are often walking with children, and these walks are great to explore with them– quite a lot of the route is friendly to little legs and pushchairs, and there are lots of diversions on the route, including playgrounds, toilets and cafes. We've had good times on sledges on the slopes of the General Cemetery, pond dipping with the Woodcraft Folk in the Botanical Gardens, playing rounders in Endcliffe Park and walking up through the woods to Forge Dam for a well deserved ice-cream or hot chocolate.

There are the landscapes of nature, the trees, the river Porter, the hills, but also the landscapes of the built environment, the fantastical monuments in the General Cemetery, and the wonderfully restored glass houses in the Botanical Gardens. Finally you will reach farmland, where today you might even see llamas as well as sheep on the moorland pastures.

Nowadays, for me, the value of this walk is the way it facilitates 'talking' walks with my women friends in particular. We can amble along, discuss all the usual topics – work, family, relationships, health, getting older, straying sometimes into recipes and clothing, sometimes into films or exhibitions we've just seen and books we've just read, while still managing to engage with what's around us and enjoy spectacular floral displays in the Botanical Gardens, or the minutiae of lichen life on a stone wall.

My second walk, by contrast, takes you into the Dark Side of the Peak District, up near the Woodhead Tunnel, and the Dunford Reservoir. This area of the Dark Peak is particularly marred and scarred by human intervention and much battered by the weather. Be warned, it is not pretty! The area has a wild beauty of its own which deserves to be explored. I've chosen this walk as the landscape carries lots of memories for me from the time when I lived here. The short

Jill's boots enjoying a rest

4-5 mile circuit described here takes you through the settlement, Townhead, from which my daughter takes her surname, and past the community, Lifespan, where she was born in the late 70s.

One of our many slogans was Nuclear Family No Thanks. We worked hard in our mixed intentional community to build alternative methods of supporting each other through (endless) discussions, our women's groups, our efforts at shared childcare and, perhaps most important to me, our endeavours to resist hierarchies or dependence, either on a man or the state.

Not surprisingly this was not easy (understatement). My time in the community was a roller-coaster ride of highs and lows. Escaping the intensity of living in an ever-changing group by walking out of the door and up and down these lanes and hills was an important survival mechanism for me. I didn't have to go very far to get fabulous sensory experiences, like the heady scent of purple heather or the scream of the wind as it tried to remove our slates or hats (or anything not tied down really) or that curious creaking rumble of snow sliding off the rooftops.

It's a very long time now since I left, and the community has shape changed and shifted even more than I have. There is not just one solitary windmill but many, and they are accompanied by solar panels as well. The toilets are still outside, but now they are composting ones. The trees planted as little slips when I lived there are now 20 feet and more high, providing shelter for the gardens and the birds. It's not just the curlew now. There are all sorts of birds to treasure, including goldfinches. The freight trains no longer disturb the peace at night, the Woodhead Tunnel is closed and the railway line at the bottom of the valley has become the Transpennine Trail, popular with walkers and cyclists. There are many more ghosts now to add to those of the navvies who lost their lives building the Woodhead Tunnel, the children who walked to the school at Carlecotes, the workers who lived in the tin town above Dunford Bridge and built the Winscar and other reservoirs, or the railway workers who lived in the terraces in Townhead and serviced the marshalling yards at the foot of the valley.

I am glad to see, though, as I walk past, that those battered old terraced houses are still in collective ownership and committed to that high but necessary ideal of sustainable living.

Boxing Day walk

SLICE OF SHEFFIELD

OS Sheffield and Barnsley Explorer 278
Start Grid reference 858342
Start point – General Cemetery
Length – varies – Cemetery to Ringinglow 5 miles
Ascent – 100 metres – can be muddy
Refreshments – Botanical Gardens, Endcliffe Park Café, Forge
Dam, Ringinglow Alpaca Visitor Centre
Public Transport – buses 3, 4 and 22 go past or near the
General Cemetery

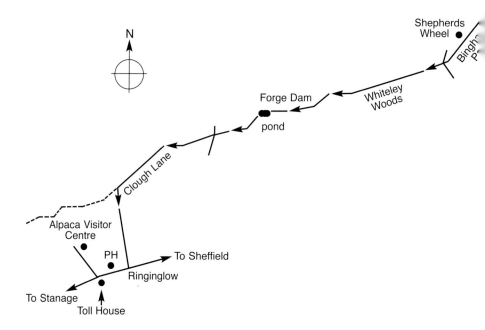

This is a walk through Sheffield's history. Start in the General
Cemetery with its many and varied monuments celebrating entrepre-
neurship, invention, religious devotion and radicalism – Samuel
Holberry, executed for his part in agitating for male suffrage is

42

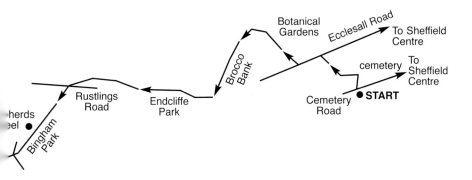

commemorated here; move on through the Botanical Gardens with their Edwardian feel and their grand nineteenth century educational purpose; on again through Endcliffe Park, established by the paternalistic City Council for the good of the people of Sheffield when it was rare for working folk to get any paid time off work at all; then you will pass the Shepherd Wheel, Wire Mill Dam and Forge Dam as well as other hammer ponds, relics of how Sheffield's industrial strength was created.

The walk is not difficult, but make sure you take care when crossing any of the roads.

- Start the walk at the Egyptian Gate of the General Cemetery on Cemetery Road. Take any path down the hill and leave by The Gatehouse. At this point you can simply do a loop round the Cemetery, down past the catacombs and back along the banks of the Porter. There are interpretative boards to give you some back ground to the monuments and wildlife to be seen in the Cemetery.

The General Cemetery, which opened in 1836, is full of architectural interest, with several listed monuments. For more details of what to see and do in the cemetery, see the website set up by the Friends of the General Cemetery: www.gencem.org

- To continue on the Slice of Sheffield walk, leave by The Gatehouse, cross Stalker Lees Road and go along Cemetery Avenue to the Ecclesall Road where you turn left, cross the road using the pelican crossing and enter the Botanical Gardens from the entrance in Thompson Road.

- The Botanical Gardens, familiarly known as the Botanics or even Tanix, are one of Sheffield's great treasures. Walk up through the gardens and leave by the Botanical Road entrance onto Brocco Bank.

- You can also follow a self contained loop in the gardens especially if you want to spot the Bear Pit, follow the Riddle Trail, explore the Glass Houses or just generally go 'Wow' at all the plants. There are toilets and a café in the gardens.

Sheffield Botanical Gardens

The gardens cover 19 acres and were first opened in 1836. Originally designed by Robert Marnock in the Gardenesque style, the site now has fifteen different garden areas featuring collections of plants from all over the world, including Mediterranean, Asian, American prairie-style, woodland and rock-and-water plantings. The Gardens contain several listed buildings including the restored Grade II* listed curvilinear Glass Pavilions, some of the earliest ever built. The gardens are usually open from dawn to dusk.

For more details ring 0114 268 6001 or see the website: www.sbg.org.uk

---

- Go left from the Botanical Road entrance and follow Brocco Bank downhill to the Hunters Bar roundabout, which still has the old toll bar on it. Use the pelican crossings make your way to the main entrance of Endcliffe Park, with its memorial to Queen Victoria and its old pavilion. At this point you are joining part of Sheffield's Round Walk – for maps and information see the website: www.sheffieldroundwalk.co.uk/

- The walk takes you through Endcliffe Park, a lovely and well-used local park, first acquired for the people of the city in the 1880s. Watch out for flying Frisbees, footballs, joggers and cyclists here. It has a popular café, toilets and plenty of space for rounders and football as well as a recently renovated playground. You are now following the valley of Porter Brook. One of Sheffield's great strengths as an early industrial city was the water power harnessed from its five main rivers as they surged down from the Peak District into the Don in the heart of the city. In its heyday, the Porter Brook alone powered 21 waterwheels, mostly used for grinding various types of the blades that made Sheffield famous. On this stretch of the walk you will see several of these industrial relics. Great efforts are now being made to clean up these waterways and restore the fish and other wildlife.

- Follow the path that goes more or less straight on until you reach a T junction where you turn right then go past (or stop at!) the play ground and the café. Shortly after there is a fork in the path, so take the right hand fork across the river. Stay on the main path until you reach Rustlings Road. You will pass two ponds both with a water fall at the dam wall and plenty of duck feeding opportunities. Cross Rustlings Rd and pass into Bingham Park at the gate near the park keeper's cottage. Follow the main path and you will pass the Shepherd Wheel. You can also see a fine array of allotments.

Shepherd Wheel

There have been water powered workshops here since at least 1584. The overshot waterwheel is powered from a large dam stocked with water diverted from the Porter Brook. The current 18th century buildings are Grade II* listed and are currently being restored. The grinding workshop finally closed in 1930.

- Cross Highcliffe Rd into Whiteley Woods. By now the walk has become a proper woodland walk. Continue on the main path until you reach Whiteley Wood Road, cross it and continue along the main path past the fishing spots of Wire Mill Dam and pond. You will eventually reach the lane at Forge Dam. Beyond Forge Dam the path is more difficult for pushchairs or wheel chairs so at this point you may choose to return to Endcliffe Park. You could also leave the walk and catch a bus back into Sheffield by turning right up the lane and going straight on up the hill until you reach Fulwood where there are frequent number 60 buses to Sheffield.

- To continue with the walk turn left and follow the main path to Forge Dam, past the children's playground with its large slide built into the hillside. There are toilets as well as a popular café here.

- The last stage on this walk takes you up through Forge Dam to Ringinglow. Carry on past the café up a narrow path and round Forge Dam. At the end of the dam the path crosses the river. Continue along the main path until the next road crossing is reached. You are now leaving urban Sheffield and reaching its rural fringes. Cross the next road and head straight on until you reach a fork in the path. You take either fork, as they both eventually join a surfaced lane, Clough Lane. Carry on along Clough Lane, until you reach a stile on your left hand side leading into a field on a steep hillside, a favourite for sledgers in winter. The path up the hill is very easy to follow. This is the route of the walk. Clough Lane meanwhile veers off to the right. Once at the top of the hill continue in a straight line over a stile built into a wall and into another field.

- Ringinglow can now be seen up ahead slightly to the right. You will come out of the fields onto Ringinglow Road. Turn right to pass the Norfolk Arms pub and view the former turnpike road out of Sheffield. You can still see the old toll house, dating from 1778, and the Norfolk Arms, an old coaching inn. Be careful on this busy road. From Ringinglow old time travellers would be tackling wild moorland to get to Chapel-en-le-Frith or Grindleford, so I'm sure a coaching halt was very welcome. You are now very close to the

Limb Brook, the old boundary between the Saxon kingdoms of Mercia and Northumbria, so you are treading very well worn paths!

- You may choose to finish the walk here and take a bus back into Sheffield, or you can walk back to Forge Dam, Endcliffe Park, the Botanical Gardens or the General Cemetery depending on your stamina, and possibly the weather! You could take time to visit the new Alpaca Centre which is along Fulwood Lane on the right. If you want an alternative way back onto Clough Lane, continue along Fulwood Lane until the first footpath sign right, which follows Porter Brook.

Tree tracery
Jill Angood

47

OS Peak District Explorer Dark Peak OL1
Start Grid reference 157023
Start point – Dunford Bridge car park
Length – 4 miles
Ascent – 80 metres
Refreshments – no refreshments available in Dunford Bridge since the Stanhope Arms closed
Public Transport: the bus stop in the car park is served by a bus service (20) linking Holmfirth bus station, Penistone High Street and Barnsley Rail Interchange

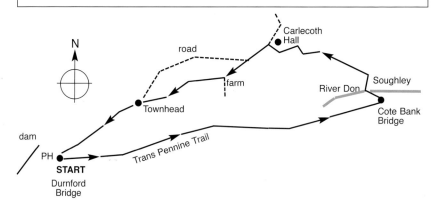

The going is mostly straightforward on this walk, but it is muddy in places, especially in the appropriately named Soughley Bottom. There is some road walking and you may encounter livestock – cows, horses and sheep as well as cyclists. The weather is often wild and wet at this height in the Pennines so make sure you have warm and water-proof clothing. The walk starts from the car park set up for the TransPennine Trail at Dunford Bridge. The TransPennine Trail (TPT) has been developed as a route for walkers, cyclists and horse riders linking the Irish and North seas between Southport and Hornsea. The section from Dunford Bridge towards Penistone follows the route of the railway that linked Sheffield and Manchester via the Woodhead

Tunnel. There is an interpretative board near the bus shelter outlining the history of the area. The railway was a significant employer, first providing work for navvies building the line and excavating the Woodhead Tunnel, and then for railway workers servicing the line.

- Go straight from the car park to the TransPennine trail and walk along the valley for about 2 miles. You follow the River Don down the valley and go past a nature reserve at Wogden Foot. Leave the trail at Cote Bank Bridge and follow the signpost to Carlecotes.

Woodhead Tunnel

There are three tunnels through the Pennines from Dunford Bridge to Longdendale. They were a massive and costly engineering achievement. More than 50 people died in the mid 19th century when the first two tunnels were completed, many as a result of cholera which swept through the shanty town where the workers lived. The last train ran through the tunnel in 1981, but one tunnel is still used for electricity cables hence the line of giant pylons in the valley.

- There is a nice picnic spot near an old bridge and ford, and then you follow a track and path up past the beautiful old farmhouse and barn at Soughley Bottom. Watch for the footpath signs, and follow the path to the left across the fields to the church of St Anne at Carlecotes.

- Go up a path with the church on your right and turn left along the Carlecotes to Dunford Bridge road after you have passed the church. You will see a very old school room on the right, now a holiday cottage. Follow the footpath signs to your left, first along a track then through the fields. This is an old paved path which is very soggy in places. Keep your eyes out for the stiles and footpath signs.

- Cross the fields with horses and come out on the track to Lower

Townhead farm. Turn left along the road to return to Dunford Bridge. You will pass through the settlement of Townhead, developed to house the railway workers. On the left are the old Coronation Street style terraced houses owned by Lifespan Community – these very urban looking houses are an odd sight in the middle of the moors – and on the right, the former school and chapel, now private houses.

- Head down the hill on the road to finish where you started, Dunford Bridge, dominated by the enormous dam built to contain Winscar Reservoir.

Living in Communities

To find out more about communal living now check out the Diggers and Dreamers website at:
www.diggersanddreamers.org.uk/
or write to Diggers and Dreamers, care of Edge of Time Ltd., BCM Edge, London WC1N 3XX for details of the directory

---

HEATHER

Heather Hunt

Born in Sheffield
but left aged 3 –
now happily
returned to be
near the hills and
enjoying my
transition from
clinical
psychologist to
outdoor
environmental
educator.

My first walk is one of the earliest I did when I came to Sheffield in 1997. I went with Sue Beardon and a new friend then, Rachel Heatley. I was bowled over by the landscapes and vistas, and intrigued by the rising forms of Crook Hill. It confirmed my decision that Sheffield was a great place to live, both for the access to magnificent walking country and for the delight in old and new friendships with women. Rachel was killed in a climbing accident in June 2000. So for me this walk is in memory of Rachel.

Before moving to Sheffield I had been introduced to the fine walking country in the Dark Peak through weekends with Red Rope, the Socialist Walking and Climbing Group, and had enjoyed walks in Edale and on Derwent Edge. However, they had remained distinct walks in fragments of the landscape, accessed by different road routes. One of the joys of this Crook Hill walk for me is how it puts the pieces of the landscape together. From Crook Hill and the ridge North West to Lockerbrook there are fine views South West towards Edale and North East to Derwent Edge with the fascinating forms of the Wheel Stones.

I have walked the area many times on my own and with different friends, in all conditions, including a snowy Christmas day when we saw brown hares below Derwent Edge and enjoyed our Christmas lunch on a bench near Ashopton looking at

51

a perfect reflection of snow clad trees in the reservoir.

I love the variety of scenes and moods of this walk – from wild boulder strewn summits of Crook Hill and open moorland with wide panoramic views, to stately, sheltered beech woods, quiet paths under Scots pines by the calm expanse of reservoir and from the Derwent Edge side, the East, particular light that seems to capture intense reflections.

My second walk reflects my enjoyment of discovering interesting countryside which is not in the National Park but which can be reached by walking from where I live. It also engages with my interest in the question of how and where we can grow more of our own food locally.

The walk starts at my second home, the Meersbrook allotment site and goes up through Gleadless Valley woods, and then over the watershed into the Moss Valley, in Derbyshire, Gleadless Valley woods are my local "green lung", a gorgeous mixture of coppice oak, beech and sycamore woodland, laced with paths and traces of history, framed by more recent housing estates. I'm learning a lot about the area from the Gleadless Valley Wild Life Group as a (not very active) ranger. The Meersbrook itself was the boundary between the ancient countries of Mercia and Northumbria. The watershed at Norton is said to be the highest point before the Urals to the East. I discovered the Moss Valley only in the last couple of years as part of exploring the arable farming land which is in walking distance from where I live.

As part of the Transition Town movement I was (and still am) motivated to explore how our communities can scale up local food growing projects for the benefit of our and the planet's health. Our local Transition initiative is now developing a Community Supported Agriculture (CSA) project on 9 acres of land in the Moss Valley. The project is called Hazelhurst Community Supported Agriculture Co-op Ltd. I am one of the founding members and very involved in getting this ambitious project off the ground, or rather, on the ground. The walk takes us past the CSA project field where we will be growing organic vegetables and fruit. The field also offers splendid south facing views.

A delight for me has been the discovery of this landscape, aided by new connections to local history and wild life groups and an oral history project I have been conducting with neighbouring farmers.

I enjoy the gentle, rolling farm-land landscape, the Moss Brook itself winding its way through magnificent bluebell woods, the abundant bird life and interesting industrial archaeology. I have discovered much about the area. "Dams," the local name for mill ponds, on the Moss are reminders of the water powered blade grinding that was part of the scythe and sickle making industry. This developed from the 14th Century and became famous throughout Europe in the 17th, 18th and 19th centuries, farming was then only the side line. Mixed farming, using rotation, became the norm from 18th to mid 20th century, sheep being the main livestock until a transition to dairy occurred around mid 20th century. Along the walk you will see that recently farmers have moved more to beef cattle with pasture and some arable with some farms providing livery and one concentrating on intensive pig farming.

Although much of the farming is now heavily chemically dependent, the farmers and their families I have talked to are deeply connected to the land, concerned about animal welfare, very knowledgeable and interested in the local wild life. They are supportive and welcoming to our organic community orientated food growing project.

The walk ends in the village of Ford.

OS Peak District Explorer Dark Peak OL1
Start Grid reference 191865
Start point – Ladybower Reservoir, junction of Snake Pass and road to Derwent Dams
Length – variable – 5·5 miles short version, 7·5 long version.
Ascent – 220 metres short version, 430 metres long version
Time – 3 hours short version, 4·5 hours long version
Refreshments – kiosk at Fairholmes, Ladybower Inn

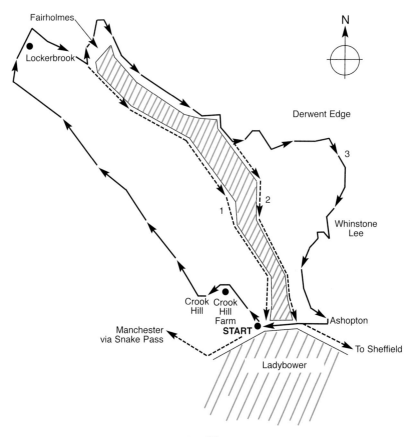

This walk is easy to do by bus 241 from the Sheffield Interchange. It goes close to the start and you can catch the bus at Ladybower Inn for return. Remember, winter services are less frequent. Cars can be parked just before the bridge near the junction of Snake Pass and the road up to Derwent Dams.

- The walk starts at this junction. A steep path goes up from the minor road to Derwent very soon after the start. The path is now diverted to skirt the right hand side of the Crookhill Farm and join the track. Here, if you want to get up onto the top of Crook Hill, divert off the track and climb straight up to the top.

- Follow the ridge over the next summit and drop down following a wall to link back up with the main footpath across to Bridge-end pasture. Go through a gate and cross over boggy pasture, following a rough path uphill to reach another gate. Keep on the highest ground across more bog until another gate takes you to the edge of a wood. This spur gives magnificent views towards Edale and to Derwent Edge.

- Continue on along the edge of the wood to a junction of many paths and tracks, where you turn right (north) to reach Lockerbrook, an outdoor pursuits centre belonging to the Woodcraft Folk which is bookable for groups. Go past Lockerbrook and take a path downhill on the right signed to Fairholmes. This passes through stately beech woods to a track onto which you turn right. Just round a bend in the track look out for the path off to the right continuing down through the woods to the road that leads to Fairholmes. Here you will find a refreshment kiosk and National Park information centre, toilets and hungry ducks. It is the fourth most visited spot in the National Park – deservedly so. There is also bike hire if you wish to take a tour by bicycle around the reservoir. You have choices here:

  1. Take the path following the west side of the reservoir back to the starting point (3·5 kilometres).

2. Return on the quiet road then bridle track on the East side of the reservoir, reached by going through Fairholmes car park and continuing past the large dam to follow the road round to the right.

3. For a much longer and tougher route, walk and continue as route two until the end of the tarmac and half a kilometre along the bridle track, just past a National Trust Farm. Take a footpath going up through a hay field that leads uphill to just below Derwent Edge. Continue south towards Whinstone Lee Tor and a junction of paths. Here turn sharp right steeply down to meet the path that continues south to Ashopton. You can return from here to the road if you have a waiting car, or keep going east on a path that goes behind the Ladybower Inn. Drop down to the Inn for buses back to Sheffield.

The history is rich and thought provoking. It was once a quiet river valley with 2 villages, Derwent and Ashopton, then in 1912 the "Tin Town" of Birchinlee grew up for 1000 "navvies" just further north than Fairholmes. They built the first two of the three dams, Howden (1912) and Derwent Dams (1916) to flood the valley and start the chain of three reservoirs to supply the growing urban water demands of Sheffield, Derby, Leicester and Nottingham. The current capacity of the reservoirs is 463,692 million litres. Ladybower reservoir was completed in 1945 which flooded the two villages of Derwent and Ashopton and residents moved to the houses built below the Ladybower Dam. The information centre at Fairholmes has a video on a loop with excellent footage of Birchinlee and information about the lost villages but nothing about any protest at the time. Just north of Fairholmes on the West side there is a tower on the dam dedicated as a museum about the Dam Busters. Any mention of the hundreds killed in Dresden is a stark omission.

Crook Hill
Jenny Fortune

Gleadless and Moss Valley blue bell walk
taking in a local community supported
<u>agriculture project</u>

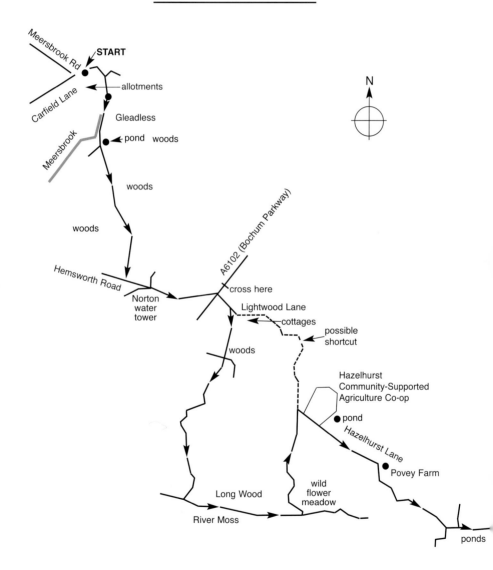

OS Sheffield and Barnsley Explorer 278.
Start Grid reference 360844
Start point – Meersbrook Allotments Gate. Junction Carrfield
Avenue and Meersbrook Road, Sheffield 8.
Finish – Bridge Inn at Ford. GR 402804
Length – 6 miles. Short version 4 miles
Ascent – 170 metres
Time – 3 and a half hours
Refreshments – Bridge Inn at Ford
Public transport – Buses from Sheffield to Meersbrook for start
of walk. Buses from Ford to Sheffield, five minutes to the hour
every day except Sunday when no service. For the short walk,
missing out Gleadless Valley, bus from Sheffield to Norton,
Hemsworth Road.

The walk is a linear one and easy to do by public transport. The 39 bus from Sheffield City Centre goes to Meerstock Road, the start of the walk.

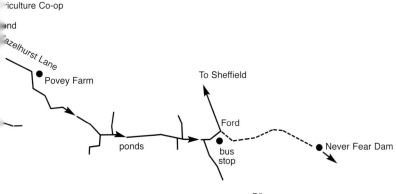

- The walk starts at the bottom gate of Meersbrook allotment site at the junction of Carrfield Avenue and Meersbrook Road. Or, if coming from Heeley Green, start at the bridge over the Meersbrook at the junction of the track from Cat Lane with the one coming in from the right from the gates.

- The first 2 kilometres is a steady ascent up Gleadless Valley to Hemsworth Road, Norton. Follow the track alongside the allotment site next to the Meersbrook. Ignore the track going off to the left after 50 metres. Follow the track going gently uphill through the woods leaving the stream to the right. Look out for the old orchard which was part of Lees Hall Farm as you approach the pond. At the pond, take the left hand fork and keep going up past the golf course to your left and Newfield School to your right. Turn round for good views back over Sheffield and beyond. The track comes out at new housing and beyond to meet Hemsworth Road.

- The next 1 kilometre is along the watershed which takes you along uninspiring pavements to the busy ring road which you cross to go into Lightwood Lane and the start of the Moss Valley. Turn left onto Hemsworth Road along the pavement a short distance to the Norton water tower roundabout. Cross directly over and take the little path to the left of the hedge and the main road. Follow Norton Avenue to the roundabout with the very busy ring road. It is advisable to walk along past the roundabout till you see central bollards to help you cross the road safely and then go back to Lightwood Lane, signed as a cul-de-sac.

- The next 3 kilometres is a loop from Lightwood Lane taking rights of way across farmland and woodland down to the Moss Brook, through blue bell woods and back up to the lane and the CSA project site. An OS map is useful here as the footpaths are not clear on the ground. To get straight to the CSA site just keep to the lane. For a more interesting walk, 200 metres down Lightwood Lane, on a left hand bend, take a footpath to the right down a track. The foot path is opposite red brick houses. There is a finger post but this is easily missed among the trees. If you pass a delightful row of old sand- stone cottages you have missed it!

- Follow the track through fields and over stiles, sometimes in poor repair, to a wood. Follow the path down to the stream and up the other side. Keep going straight on and out of the wood. The main path on the ground veers left downhill through the wood. Don't take it. At the next field junction keep straight on, keeping the hedge to your right with woods below you to the left. The map marks a junction of rights of way at this point but the paths are not clear on the ground.

- At the next field boundary veer slightly right into the next field and cross the field diagonally South West to where Hazelbarrow Farm can be seen nestling among some trees. The footpath goes round the farm buildings, now used for livery, passing the farm cottage on the right. This farm and its 200 acres of land is owned by Sheffield City Council and is farmed by several generations of a tenant farming family.

- At the edge of the farm take the footpath down the hill to the right. Don't take the signed track straight on through a field gate. Follow the path through fields (where lapwings are often seen) and into the woods. Follow a path down to the stream. This is the Moss and Long Wood, the beginnings of miles of bluebell woodland, paths and bridle ways. This walk follows a path to the left of the stream going downstream. The path is clear on the ground but not marked on the map. Follow the stream through the wood for 1 kilometre. The path then comes out into a wild flower meadow.

- This is the point you turn left uphill away from the stream. Next, take a path at the side of a field, ploughed or with arable crop, adjacent to a wood on your right. You are going north now. Zig zag down to the stream and cross a little bridge. Come out of the woodland and continue uphill on a clear path alongside a diverse and bushy hedge. The field to the right of this one is where the open cast mine was in 1957. The larch and birch wood on the hill to the right of the field is a plantation planted on the spoil heap. Follow the path up to the lane. Turn right down the lane 100 metres. You will see a hedge neatly laid on the left on the other side of which is a small pond. The gate to the left of this is the entrance to the CSA site.

A bit about the Community Supported Agriculture site. You are welcome to take a look around the site. At the time of writing, May 2010, these are the plans. The field next to the road is going to be a community fruitery with fruit trees and soft fruit bushes and is managed by a Quaker company. The larger field, accessed by a path alongside the pond, is going to be for organically grown vegetables for the benefit of local communities in Heeley Meersbrook and local to the site. Currently the land is owned by the Quaker property company and we are planning to launch a community share issue to raise money to purchase the land and fund the necessary infrastructure such as a bore hole for water, wind mill to pump it up, polytunnels and secure storage. Enjoy a walk up to the top of the field, keeping to the hedgerow, which is a great picnic spot with good views south.

- The final stretch to Ford is about 3 kilometres. GR 402804. There is a choice of routes, over the fields NW from Povey Farm (where you can buy farm butchered and made pork sausages) keeping to the side of Ryall's wood, passing interesting history about scythe and sickle making and joining Sloane Lane to go down into Ford. Or, follow the slightly shorter and easier route marked on the map, and continue down Hazelhurst Lane past Povey Farm continuing as a bridle way for 1 kilometre down to the Moss. Don't cross the Moss but keep to the track to the left of the Moss which turns into a road passing Geerlane and Birley Hay Farms and mill ponds. This track leads into the road which takes you straight into Ford. You will pass the bus stop before you reach the Bridge Inn, itself on a mill pond and the end of the walk.

- However, if you want more, there is a well marked path following the Moss downstream of Ford, through lush meadow which takes you to "Never Fear Dam" and 2 kilometres further on through more lovely woodland to a beam engine house which was a pumping station for a coal mine.

Gleadless Valley Wildlife Group. Enquiries 0114 281 1327

Moss Valley Wild Life Group. Secretary 0114 248 0529

Transition Sheffield www.transitionsheffield.org.uk

Hazelhurst Community Supported Agriculture Co-op Ltd. www.hazelhurst.coop

Ford and the Ford Valley. An observation of life at Ford from the earliest records to the height of its industries. Amos Bright

CATHY

When I was nine I planned to live a long way from anywhere and keep cows. Somehow I got distracted by the public sector and motherhood but now, aged 52, I'm back on track!

These three walks are part of the 100 mile route I designed around Sheffield. The walk formed itself in my mind as I was considering how to celebrate my 50th birthday. Although I was born and brought up in South London I realised that I had spent nearly half my life in Sheffield and that Sheffield felt much more like home than London suburbs ever had. Approaching 50, a busy professional with children growing up and moving on, my life was changing and I felt in need of a period of retreat. A long distance walk seemed like a good idea, but when I started to think about which long distance walk I might do I realised that I also wanted to do something that celebrated and marked the extent to which Sheffield had become my home. And so the idea of a long distance walk that started and finished at my own front door was born.

I bought local OS maps and laid them out on my living room floor. Then, cutting a piece of string to the equivalent of 100 miles, I traced a 100 mile round walk, along tracks and footpaths, from my home, around the north west of Sheffield, up across and through the Dearne Valley with its coal mining history, down into the Dukeries of north Nottinghamshire and round through Chesterfield and the edge of north Derbyshire's Peak District, before eventually heading back into Sheffield and home again.

The walk took me six days and through

an extraordinary diversity of landscape sculpted by centuries of changing human use. It was not, perhaps, the most beautiful walking that I have ever done but it was certainly amongst the most fascinating, and connected me with the human history of South Yorkshire, North Nottinghamshire and North Derbyshire in a striking and powerful way.

On the second to last day, walking along the Chesterfield Canal, I found myself humming a forgotten song from way back in my child-hood......:

WHAT is this life if, full of care,
We have no time to stand and stare?—

No time to stand beneath the boughs,
And stare as long as sheep and cows:

No time to see, when woods we pass,
Where squirrels hide their nuts in grass:

No time to see, in broad daylight,
Streams full of stars, like skies at night:

No time to turn at Beauty's glance,
And watch her feet, how they can dance:

No time to wait till her mouth can
Enrich that smile her eyes began?

WH Davies

LODGE MOOR TO OUGHTIBRIDGE

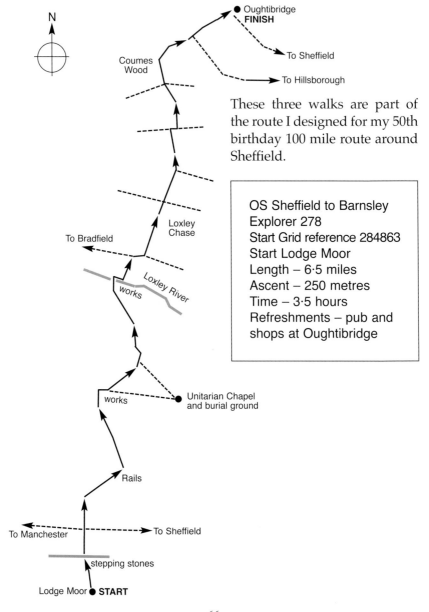

These three walks are part of the route I designed for my 50th birthday 100 mile route around Sheffield.

OS Sheffield to Barnsley Explorer 278
Start Grid reference 284863
Start Lodge Moor
Length – 6·5 miles
Ascent – 250 metres
Time – 3·5 hours
Refreshments – pub and shops at Oughtibridge

- The number 51 bus goes to the terminus at Lodge Moor frequently from Sheffield Centre. At the terminus continue to walk westwards, crossing the road and taking the first footpath down to the right. As the path bends round to the left, in just a few metres there are way marks. Find here a narrow path going steeply down to the right through the birch woods. Towards the bottom of this path there are some wooden steps leading down to stepping stones. If the Rivelin brook is swollen some of the stones will be submerged, and all of them are a little slippery, so tread carefully across to a path on the far side, on which you turn right. This takes you past the Filter House to the main A57 road.

- Cross the road and take the footpath opposite. This is not used much so will not be that obvious. It goes along the wall to a gate which is tied up, but just to the right of it a stone stile goes over the wall. Cross the next large steeply sloping field diagonally to the right and at the top corner find a stile over the fence, depositing you on a footpath. Go right on this. The path will soon become a small lane and the houses of Rails come into view. Take the first footpath left, signposted Stopes.

- Keep following this until reaching Riggs High Road. Cross the road and take the path opposite that goes downhill to arrive at the Stannington/Dungworth Road near a factory with a large chimney. Turn right going past the factory. If you wish to visit the Unitarian chapel and graveyard, keep going on this road going uphill for about one kilometre and it is on your left. This is a beautiful building and a peaceful spot with a great view to the next part of the walk. From there you can continue a short way and take Spoon Lane going left downhill to Storrs Brook. If you decide not to visit the chapel, take the first footpath on the left of the road, opposite the factory. There is a large circular flattened area with a notice about CCTV. Keep between that and the road and the path goes between bushes. At what looks like an old airshaft keep downhill and you will see the path going diagonally down, keeping roughly with the stream below. Keep in this direction, the path not always being very clear, to a signpost where the stream meets with Spoon Lane.

- Go left here steeply uphill. This is a gorgeous place where you will see herons and other birds, and on a lovely day might prove to be an excellent picnic spot.

- The lane reaches the road, where you turn right, still steeply uphill. At the sharp bend right find a footpath that goes past a little terrace of houses and bends round them to the left, past a field of horses. Keep to the left of the horse field and cross the stile, but instead of following the waymark straight ahead, cross the field diagonally down to the right to arrive at a stile. Cross and follow this path down towards Loxley Valley.

- Take a path through a gate and then take the first path going right at a right angle down steps to disused factory buildings. Follow the path past the fenced off buildings and at the bottom turn right and follow the road round as it bends left and uphill again. At the road turn right and very soon take a footpath going left through a large gate. In a couple of hundred metres the footpath veers off the track which continues to houses and over a stile. Follow this path, which keeps with a small culvert all the way up to Myers Lane.

- Cross the road and continue on a path passing some woods and finally arriving at Stubbing Lane. Keep straight on along the road ahead, keeping to the road until it reaches another road close to a large school. Turn right here and take the first footpath to the left, signed Onesacre, keeping on this, going roughly north until reaching another small road near a house. Go right here and after the farm track on the left look out for a stile and footpath sign. Cross the stile and go downhill towards Coumes Brook and Coumes Wood. This is another very pretty stretch of the walk.

- At the lane, turn right and keep walking until it meets the road down to Oughtibridge. The buses back to Sheffield actually come up here so you can look out for a bus stop on the opposite side of the road as you go downhill. Or you can walk right down to the village and the River Don, pubs and shops and catch the bus there. The numbers 57 and 58 go back to Sheffield.

Derbyshire tree
Jill Angood

OUGHTIBRIDGE TO WORTLEY

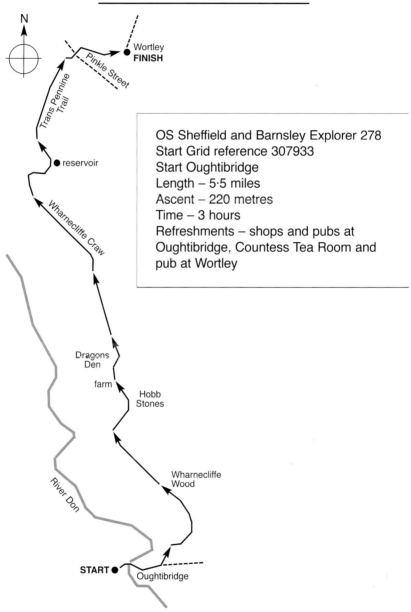

N

Wortley
FINISH

Pinkle Street

Trans Pennine Trail

reservoir

Wharncliffe Crag

OS Sheffield and Barnsley Explorer 278
Start Grid reference 307933
Start Oughtibridge
Length – 5·5 miles
Ascent – 220 metres
Time – 3 hours
Refreshments – shops and pubs at
Oughtibridge, Countess Tea Room and
pub at Wortley

Dragons
Den

farm

Hobb
Stones

Wharncliffe
Wood

River Don

START ●
Oughtibridge

57 and 58 buses go to Oughtibridge from Sheffield Centre every quarter of an hour, either from the Interchange or from Castlegate.

- When you get off at Oughtibridge, cross over the river in the direction of Grenoside and continue walking up the road, past the playground and the Pheasant public house. Cross the railway and immediately take a path to the left going alongside the grounds of a factory. The path goes along a wall for a while and then slightly uphill to meet a track. Turn right along the far side of the factory and then straight on into Wharncliffe Woods.

- Take the track going ahead not the waymarked Transpennine trail going left. Sough Dike is on your right. 400 metres from the factory there is a junction of tracks where you go straight on and take the left fork, ignoring waymark signs. At the very next junction go left. A field with cows and sheep is on your right and forest to the left. After another 400 metres there is a crossroads of tracks where you go straight on. Look to your left to see the waterfall tumbling down through the trees.

- Keep following yellow waymark posts, ignoring paths to the right until after about 15 minutes you will see the wall coming to meet your track. A short track right leads to a stile in the wall, which you cross into Wharncliffe Chase. Go straight on up the path, past a radio mast with Hobbs Stones ahead. The path swings left towards buildings, which you head towards, finally going through a gate and into the farm yard.

- Continue on the track until a gate, which you do not go through. Instead look for a small path heading left through the trees to reach the edge of Wharncliffe Crags. Go right on the edge path and stay on this all the way along Wharncliffe Edge. The path drops a little keeping to the edge, and past lovely mossy rocks and a couple of streams, until meeting up again with the wall at the top. Keep on this main path, ignoring paths off into Wharncliffe Heath to the right. You will soon see views of Stocksbridge and the steel works ahead. The path bends round to the right and downhill through a gate into woodland. Soon you come to a small pond with a dam. Follow the pond round to the left, past some wooden steps which you ignore, over the dam and meet a wide track.

The crags are the venue of the legend of the Dragon of Wantley, a myth that was made into a 17th century satirical poem and an opera by Henry Carey. The legend was mentioned by Sir Walter Scott in the opening chapter of *Ivanhoe*, "Here haunted of yore the fabulous Dragon of Wantley". The story tells the tale of how More, of More Hall, slays a troublesome dragon which lives on the crags. A cave at the southern end of the crags, close to Wharncliffe Lodge, is called the Dragons Den and is thus marked on maps.

- Turn left here and continue on it until it meets up with the TransPennine Trail. Keep straight on and go through the underpass under the main road. Immediately through the underpass take the right fork, not the Upper Don trail to the left. Go uphill on this track, towards buildings, passing a riding school and houses to reach Finkle Street. Cross the road and slightly to the right is a foot path paved with flag stones all the way up to Wortley Church and village.

- There is a pub, village store and tea shop at Wortley. Buses go regularly to Deepcar where you can change onto the bus to Sheffield, and there is an occasional straight through bus to Sheffield from Wortley.

WORTLEY TO ELSECAR

OS Sheffield and Barnsley Explorer 278
Start Grid reference 307993
Start Wortley
Length – 7 miles
Ascent – negligible
Time – 4 hours
Refreshments – Wortley and Elsecar Heritage Centre

● From Wortley take the Timberland trail that goes past the post office and to the right of the entrance to Wortley Hall. A wide track goes all the way across to meet Carr Lane. You are on the highest ground around for a way, so the views are splendid. Keep on the track all the way to the road. Carr Lane takes you in the same direction, roughly east north east towards Pilley. When you reach the first houses you will soon come to a junction of roads at which a footpath goes off right into woods. This path is signed "alternative route, walkers only". It takes you pleasantly through Potter Holes Plantation, and is not marked on the O/S map. The path emerges from the wood onto a viewpoint with a well placed

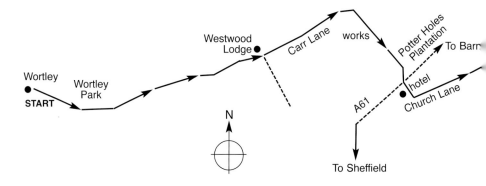

74

seat. Views from here can be had over Birdwell and beyond. Soon after this clearing the path goes into woodland again very close to the A61. Take the path going right to meet the road near to the Tankersley Manor Hotel.

- Cross the main road with care, near to a little tea van, and continue left up Church Lane, that goes up the side of the hotel. There are many alternative routes in this part of the walk, all loops of the Transpennine trail. At the far end of Church Lane is St. Peter's Church. Far reaching views can be seen from the churchyard looking south and east, so it is well worth stopping here. Across the M1 can be seen the Church spire at Wentworth. On the wooded hill to its left is the Hoober Stand, a 100ft high watchtower. The large pillar you can see to the SSE just on the edge of Rotherham is Keppel's column (GR 389946).

- The area you pass through now is fascinating. All around are mounds which show the presence of old bell pits, ancient workings to mine iron stone. As you walk down Black Lane away from the Church towards the motorway, you will see these mounds on the Tankersley Park golf course ahead. Passing under the motorway the woods to your left, Bell Ground, are the location for yet more

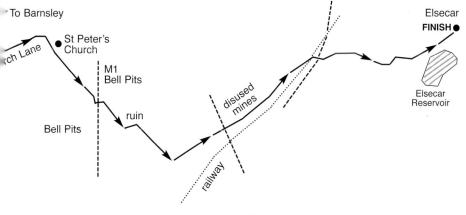

bell pits. The track arrives at a large farm with the ruins of an old Hall next to it. Pass left and right around the ruins. Notice the stone wall along this track on the right has black rocks with holes in decorating it. These are examples of clinker, the left over fused rocks from the iron smelting furnaces, sometimes locally known as crozzle.

- At the next cross roads of tracks go left, through a small stile to enter disused coal mining ground. At the main road just past a modern housing development, cross over to a garage and go straight on over through birch woods that have colonised the old mining area. When the path arrives at Stead Lane, go right and immediately left into more woods. Keep on the main path and when it forks take the right hand fork towards a stile and an open patch of field on your right. The path soon drops down to a stream and goes under power lines. Go up steps the other side and turn right onto a track. This soon crosses the railway line. When you reach the road, turn left and take the right fork up a lane to Alderthwaite Farm. The path is signed to go round the back of the farm, to its left. Soon the path strikes out across a planted field, and where it meets a field boundary with bushes, take the left fork that crosses to Skiers Hall.

- At the track go left and take the first path right, marked with a couple of arrows. This is the Barnsley boundary walk. Follow it to the north of Elsecar reservoir and continue in the same direction until reaching the Elsecar Heritage Centre. Don't go in the entrance to the right, which is the car park. Turn left, going past the public house, down a lane right with bollards at the entrance and the Heritage centre entrance is on your left. There is a very good and competitively priced tea shop just by the entrance.

- From Elsecar you can either take the train back to Sheffield – the station is up the road towards Hoyland (B6097), about 500 metres – there are buses to Chapeltown and from there buses into Sheffield. Trains go once an hour on weekdays.

Totley Brook
Sally Goldsmith

SALLY

Sally Goldsmith

Poet, songwriter, broadcaster and a bit of a wuss as a walker, though I've lived and pottered around Sheffield for 30 years

Moving up north in 1979, I exchanged the anarchy of Kings Cross for the even wilder anarchy of a life 1000 feet up on a bleak moor near Dunford Bridge. There I joined the motley of communal life at Lifespan Community – meeting one of the other contributors to this book, Jill, and like her, giving birth at home to my child – not an experience I would necessarily recommend! I developed a definite taste for that un-manicured landscape of bleary moors, stalking pylons and slurring lapwings.

When my son was tiny and we were living in Sheffield, we would usually get the bus or train out into the Peak at a weekend and do three miles or so (not bad when you're only three years old) – always with a café at the end as bait. I have kept walking out of the city all the years I've lived here but, despite romantic notions of taking off into the wild, I have never been a great success at what I would call really rugged walking. I once tried to do the Coast to Coast by myself and had to give up in agony after 3 days. What a wimp.

About 10 years ago I made a little show of songs out of what I learned from walking in the South Yorkshire Peak with groups of older ramblers. It was called *As We Walked Out* and in the process, I met people who had been campaigning for public access to wild places for most of their lives. I learned to respect just what they – and others before them – had done for the likes of you and me. A little later, the Ramblers Association commissioned a song called *Trespassers Will be Celebrated* and I pictured all those people through history toiling up the hill together:

> … See campaigners through the ages
> Walk together side by side
> Watt Tyler, Benny Rothman hand in hand
> Carpenter, Winstanley and the Diggers on the hill
> The commoners who dared to seize the land
> Stephen Morton, Barbara Castle,
> Bert Ward and Terry Howard
> The Greenham women cutting down the fence
> Elsie Gaskell and the Buntings, young Woodcraft singers too,
> Tom Stephenson, McColl and Thomas Spence …

The two walks I have chosen to describe here couldn't be more different – yet both within striking distance of my home in Totley on the southern edge of Sheffield. One consists of ancient woods, deep hedged tracks, and old stone halls, the other takes you across open boggy moor and more distant history.

OS Peak District Explorer White Peak OL24
Start Grid reference 313800
Start point – Co-op, Baslow Road, Totley
Length – 3 miles (short version); 4·5miles (longer version)
Ascent – 100 metres
Time – 1·5 hours (short version); 2·5 hours (longer version)
Refreshments – Pubs in Totley or Café next to Co-op

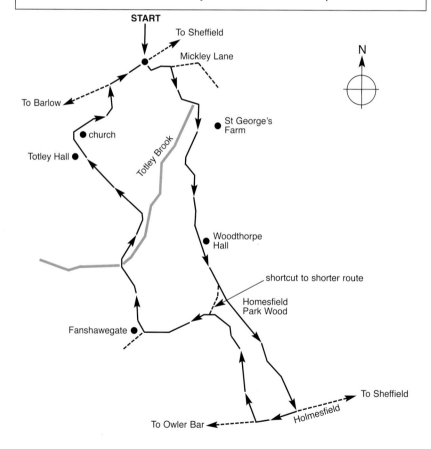

This is the default dog walk on my home patch that I take, straight out of our back door, several times a week. I often fashion it with variations which, with a good OS map, should be no bother.

One of my favourite poets, John Clare, was a farm labourer. Clare loved nothing more than to ferret and footle around his own home patch – the countryside around his village of Helpston, Northampton-shire. Not only a poet, but one of the first naturalists, he seemed to know every nest, badger's set and copse. Although I can only aspire to be as good a poet or naturalist as Clare, I understand the attractions of this. I'm never bored because daily the theatre of the place changes – the different lighting schemes of sun and weather, the varying cast of characters and animals with walk-on parts. I find that forging a real emotional connection by walking and re-walking, even in urban settings, can awaken the awareness of threats to the landscape – inappropriate development, dangers to wildlife, the destruction of historical or architectural features, light pollution – and the evidence to fight them.

Clare lived at a time of great landscape change forced upon the countryside and its people by the enclosure of the commons. He wrote about this often, even taking on the voice of the land itself, as in this extract from *The Lament of Swordy Well*:

> The silver springs grown naked dykes
> Scarce own a bunch of rushes;
> When grain got high the tasteless tykes
> Grubbed up trees, banks and bushes,
> And me, they turned me inside out
> For sand and grit and stones
> And turned my old green hills about
> And picked my very bones.

There have been lots of more recent attempts to pick the bones of our own city fringes. This walk takes in some of that land.

- Take the 97 bus from Sheffield City Centre to the Co-op on Baslow Road, Totley. Walk round the corner down Mickley Lane and enter

Greenoak Park by an old oak tree, often full of finches. Walk through the park, turning left out of it and along the path which skirts the bottom, coming onto council housing on Greenoak Road where Bill Keane, the last of the Kinder Mass Trespassers lived. Turn left here, then right onto Aldam Road.

Bill Keane was the last of the Sheffield ramblers on the 1932 Kinder Mass Trespass. This event highlighted the clamour for access to the moors – so tantalisingly out of reach to all those eager young workers from the industrial conurbations of the North. Out of this campaigning came the National Parks, eventually the Countryside and Rights of Way Act and with it the right to walk, climb and cycle freely in much of our countryside. In 2002, we took Bill to the 70th anniversary of the Mass Trespass at Hayfield where everyone seemed to be fawning over the Duke of Devonshire who'd come to apologise for the acts of his ancestors. Bill stood up, insisted on having his say too and gave due respect to the masses of unsung campaigners, many of them women, who beavered away lobbying and organising – as well as trespassing. He died later that year.

- A few yards along Aldam Road turn left at a footpath sign. Slip through the gap by the five bar gate and take the path straight ahead past the Scout Hut. It goes over a little bridge across the Totley Brook. At the top of the bank we turn right onto what is locally known as The White Lane.

Edward Carpenter. I am often aware of walking in the footsteps of important radical thinkers – writers, socialists, anarchists and feminists of the Victorian age – who got off the train at Dore and Totley Station, walked along The White Lane, up the ancient medieval holloways to Holmesfield and down to Millthorpe to meet the sandal wearing socialist sage of Sheffield and Derbyshire, Edward Carpenter. He held court there on his little smallholding where, at the time of the Wilde trial, he lived openly with his lover George Merrill.

- As you walk along The White Lane, up to your left on the small escarpment you will see Ruskin's St. George's Farm. Soon the track crosses a culverted stream coming in to join the Totley Brook – this is the boundary between Yorkshire and Derbyshire. Long tailed tits are often busy along this stretch in winter, warblers in Spring.

St George's Farm was bought by John Ruskin, the great cultural mind of the Victorian era, who set up a communal fruit growing venture there for Sheffield workers. The fruit wouldn't grow and they all fell out!

- At a division of tracks, we take the medieval tree and hedge lined holloway branching left. (The lane straight ahead up to Woodthorpe Hall has the better views but is private – although they seem pretty relaxed about it). Along our way, there are actually two almost parallel tracks – the lower one gets rather muddy in bad weather but is the most enticing and atmospheric. Look out for the really unusual old stone cobbled paving in many places.

The holloway
Duck, and you're fed inside
this oak-soaked dark -
a gullet carved from wildwood where
a pheasant's broken clockwork startles.

You're breathed in.
Only rattled blackbirds breach
the arched green hush
where banks are mossed.
Soft earth, hard stone,
leaf-litter, flesh the floor,
and still you are flowed, a boat,
runnelled and cundy borne,
away from heat that frets
in a future – not of your choosing,
yet somehow of your making.

Sally Goldsmith

- We come out at Woodthorpe Hall and take the lane straight ahead. Woodthorpe Hall is said to have been built in the seventeenth century with stone taken from Fanshawegate Hall. There are many varieties of small birds up here, including goldcrests and nuthatches. I've seen fieldfares and redwings in winter. Lovely views of the ancient fields patchworking over the hill below Totley Moss.

- For the shorter walk, pass the entrance to Holmesfield Park Wood. However, if you want a longer one, take this path through the wood and up to Holmesfield Church, turn right along the main road in Holmesfield and at the edge of the village turn right down the old shady holloway known, creepily, as Hob Lane (rather than the parallel field path) and back to Fanshawegate Lane.

Holmesfield Park Wood is full of bluebells in Spring and is green with holly at any time of year. It was originally a medieval deer park and still has its original banking and boundaries which kept the deer in and other animals out. You can see this clearly as you come back along Hob Lane – which was itself part of an important north-south route from Sheffield and Dore onto Holmesfield and through on south past Rumbling Street. It has been worn deeply over the years by the passage of feet, horses and carts.

- Carry on up Fanshawegate Lane until you come to the lovely Fanshawegate Hall. Our path goes immediately right through the old stackyard, but it's worth detouring a little further along the lane to the gateways of the house to peer through at the gardens and the arrangement of the dovecot and the old stone buildings. A tranquil place.

Fanshawegate Hall. Mr and Mrs Ramsden have lovingly restored the old house, gardens, cottage, dovecot and tithe barn at Fanshawegate. Mrs Ramsden opens her wonderful garden several times every spring and summer under the National Garden Scheme. Her cakes are pretty special too. The Hall was owned for seven centuries by the Fanshawe family – Lady Ann Fanshawe, wife of a prominent royalist, wrote a journal which was used as the stimulus for a Channel 4 drama about the Civil War, *The Devil's Whore*. The Hall became a rather scruffy farm by the turn of the nineteenth and twentieth centuries and was tenanted. To my delight, I discovered that George Adams, a working class artist who had made sandals with Edward Carpenter, lived here with his family at that time and drew the hall. I found his drawing in the early 19th century reprint of Lady Ann's journal. When he left, he moved to the new town of Letchworth Garden City which was a hotbed of cranky socialists and Victorian new-agers!

- Take the footpath past the pond and the old ash tree, through two gates and down the side of the fields (taking in a stile) towards Gillfield Wood. Again watch out for fieldfares in winter. There are lovely views here across Totley to the moors. At the bottom of the field, cross another stile – my favourite entrance into Gillfield Wood. Cross the bridge and up the bank turning right onto the main path through this long wood which follows the Totley Brook and the Derbyshire/Yorkshire boundary.

Gillfield Wood, like Holmesfield Park Wood, is officially an ancient wood, although it was sadly replanted with American oak and larch in the 1950's or 60's. It still has some of its original flora though – plenty of bluebells and wood anemones in Spring. You can also find in both woods some curious hollows – the remains of old "Q pits" – where wood was burned to make not charcoal but "whitecoal" which was used to smelt lead. Whitecoal has not been made for at least 2 centuries – and there is no-one left alive who knows quite how it was done.

- Follow the path until you come to a definite fork. Take the path to the left leading to a stile. Once over the stile keep along the side of the field towards Totley Hall. There are lots of characterful old oak trees in the field boundaries here. You will see Totley Hall, now flats, surrounded by modern housing ahead. You come out onto Totley Hall Lane. Go straight along here past the modern housing estates to find some of what is left of Totley village – old farm buildings and cottages, a Victorian lodge to the Hall and an 1830's school house. Turn right into the entrance to the church grounds, veer round past the church and onto the suburban Sunnyvale Road. Instead of turning onto Sunnyvale Road, walk straight ahead along Sunnyvale Avenue and turn left round the corner onto Main Avenue. At the main Baslow Road turn right and back to the Co-op – and maybe the friendly café next door where you can have a cuppa!

Dovecote Fanshawegate
Sally Goldsmith

Hob Lane
Sally Goldsmith

BIG MOOR

OS Peak District Exlorer White Peak OL24
Start Grid reference 275783
Starting point – Barbrook Bridge, B6054
Length – 7 miles
Ascent – 120 metres
Time – 4 hours
Refreshments – none. Nearest pub is The Peacock at Owler Bar.

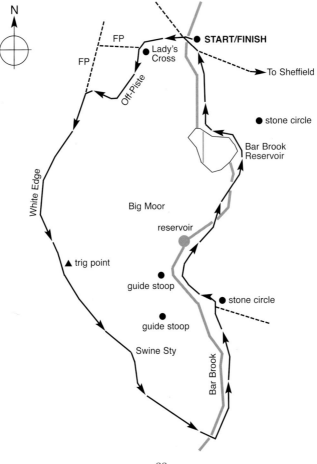

"It is big and brown, wide and drear, featureless and lonely, flat and boggy as any moor in Peakland, and yet, to those who know it most intimately, full of interest, and, in the treading of it, verily, a big man's moor." GHB Ward, Sheffield Clarion Ramblers' Handbook 1927/28.

Big Moor was certainly boggy on the soaking Saturday that us big women – Sue, Debby, Jill and I – set out with maps and compasses to practice our navigation skills. But first, after parking the car, we had to get across the raging torrent which had established itself between the road and the stile. That achieved we began an adventurous day out on what, despite its nearness to Sheffield, is a desolate, wild place.

It wasn't always so, however. Back around 2000 BC, before the peat formed, lots of people lived and farmed here – and you may be able to find evidence of their agriculture, burial places and stone circles dotted all over the moor. Not only that – there is evidence of more recent history when the moor was a difficult place to navigate for the packhorses coming across from beyond the Derwent through Curbar Gap to Chesterfield and Sheffield. GHB "Bert" Ward – known as the "King of the Ramblers" (and the very devil of a trespasser), researched many of the ancient tracks and holloways across the moor, and the guide stoops and crosses which guided them.

The walk as described is not the walk we actually did. Being big brave women (ha Bert!) we took lots of detours to discover cairns, circles and guide posts, but then found ourselves on the west bank of Barbrook on very wet ground – not recommended. However, if the weather is reasonable you might want to be adventurous yourself – so there are grid references for some of the historical features in case you should want to take them in as detours.

There may also be much to interest the wildlife fans among you – stonechats, whinchats, curlews, water birds around the reservoir. And once we turned round to see ourselves being gawped at from afar by a little group of red deer. Stunning.

- From Barbrook Bridge (GR 275783), go across the stile onto Big Moor. The path goes west uphill towards White Edge. On the left of the path about 400 metres from the start is the stump of Lady's Cross.

A **Lady's Cross** here (GR 272782) is first mentioned in a document of 1263. It is said to have served as a marker for the junction of the boundaries of Baslow, Homesfield and Totley (chiselled on it on one side are the letters I.R. 1618, on another MB meaning Manor of Baslow and on another the letter T for Totley). Bert Ward had the theory that the monks of Beauchief Abbey erected it to mark the western boundary of their free grazing, though others disagree. Lady Crosses were often places where a weary traveller could say a prayer – and rest a while.

- The path continues up onto White Edge, although we took a bearing across the moor to find the marked cairn. There wasn't much to see there, but there was a clear mound that marked the site. From here we followed the wall back to White Edge near the Hurkling Stone and then turned left onto the Edge all the way along it to the trig point and beyond.

Hurkling is a fantastic old word meaning crouching – rather like hunkering I suppose – just right for this low natural feature here which has been used as a boundary marker. On it are the initials MB for manor of Baslow and H for Holmesfield. The wall nearby was erected at the time of the nineteenth century parliamentary enclosures.

- Our next detour was onto the top of the rocky area known as Swine Sty (GR 271750) although the main path stays below it.

Swine Sty. David Hey, the great historian of Derbyshire and the Peak, says that excavation of this site has helped our under-standing of farming in the Bronze Age. A small group of buildings here were probably timber framed and thatched with turf or heather. The surrounding fields were small like gardens but hard work to clear and cultivate. When the climate changed and peat began to spread they would have been abandoned.

- We went looking for two stone guide posts or stoops dating from the 18th century, one at GR 273754, where a Bronze Age field system is marked on the ordnance survey map, and another at GR 274758, just by a stream. A path does go along here, crossing this and other streams, but disappears into bog where the little reservoir south of Barbrook reservoir comes into view. It was an exceptionally wet day when we tried it, so maybe in other conditions it is better. Somehow I doubt it.

Guide Stoops. People had a lot of trouble finding their way before the advent of the turnpike roads – and Big Moor must have been particularly difficult. An act of parliament laid down that guide posts were to be erected to aid travellers and those around Derbyshire were erected in the early 18th century. The spelling on them is often strange and wonderful – SHEFEILD, TIDSWALL, CHASTERFELD. There are around six on Big Moor.

- After exploring Swine Sty and looking for the guide stoops, it's best to follow the path down almost to the road. It is then possible to get across Bar Brook and pick up a path that follows it on the eastern side. There is an ancient slab bridge here. Keep going uphill when you get into the wooded area to reach the main track to Barbrook reservoir. Not far along this track, up to the right, there is a small stone circle – Barbrook I – with a clear path leading to it. A large cairn at GR 279757 and another stone circle – Barbrook II GR 277758 – are nearby and worth a detour too.

The Barbrook Stone Circles and cairns are evidence of a thriving Bronze Age farming community here. Barbrook I is easy to find with 13 stones, none larger than 3 feet high. Some have cup marks carved on them. There are several burial cairns nearby – in fact if you look the whole landscape is littered with them. The largest is about 50 metres to the north east. The uprights of Barbrook II stone circle – about 300 metres to the north – are unusually set within a low stone wall. Barbrook III north of the reservoir is a large circle but with very small stones.

- After this, keep following the track past the little reservoir, then crossing the brook to arrive at buildings close to Barbrook reservoir itself. The track continues along to the eastern side of the reservoir. Ignore the track to the right that goes to the road (although there is another guide stoop here if you want to detour). Barbrook III – the third stone circle is marked on the map at GR 283774. Otherwise, continue around the reservoir path and through a gate, following the path along the eastern side of the brook and up to the road. Turn left and return to your car.

Old oak tree, Totley Hall Farm
Sally Goldsmith

Jenny's
Don watershed adventure

Jenny Patient

"Young-at heart woman seeks natural connection and a chance to slow down, in and around her adopted home city."

The idea of this route was to walk along the western watershed of the Don and its Sheffield tributaries, the Little Don, Ewden Beck, Loxley, Rivelin, Porter Brook and Sheaf. In fact, I only got as far as the Ladybower Inn.

It had been a tricky summer – short of money, short of fine weather, short of holidays. Now the August Bank Holiday loomed before me, and I had no commitments to deter me from a trip. No company either, and still limited funds, and no plan in place a few days before. Heather had lent me guide books and maps for the Cleveland Way, so I'd started to think about a backpacking trip. But why waste time travelling to North Yorkshire, when Sheffield is so close to wild and beautiful places? I reached for the map and looked for a project!

Woods, water and hills are the stuff Sheffield is made of, under its superficial skin of buildings. The five rivers that define the city are the Don, and its tributaries the Loxley, Rivelin, Porter Brook and Sheaf. The idea that came to me was to walk around them, encircling the land to the west of the city where our rivers gather their water. I would start in the north, and follow the hills south, so that a raindrop rolling over my left foot would flow into Sheffield, and a raindrop on my right foot would end up in someone else's river. With little more than

93

Bivvying at the edge of the wood
Jenny Fortune

this romantic notion to guide me I packed my rucksack.

Wild camping and bivouacking were fairly new to me, but I'd had enough recent experience to know what I'd most need, and what I could leave behind. I took a sleeping bag and bivvy bag, a camping mat, an extra layer of warm clothes and waterproofs, my little camping stove and enough food for a couple of days. (My best tip on the food is to take a big piece of butter and some mushrooms and garlic – more or less any stodge tastes great with some garlic mushrooms!) What I later wished I'd remembered were the chlorine tablets that make water safe to drink – without them I had to be very careful where I collected drinking water, and boil it whenever possible.

I caught the train to Denby Dale on the Friday afternoon – it seemed to be full of Barnsley teenagers heading home from Meadowhall, and I felt sorry for them. Maybe some of them were watching the solitary, scruffy woman with the bulging rucksack, and either feeling sorry for me, or glimpsing a different way to spend the weekend?

On many walks, this one included, I've found the first hundred metres the most challenging – or maybe it's just my embarrassment at standing at the station or the bus stop trying to make the map, the compass and my surroundings agree with each other! After a grand tour of the station environs, I got the hang of it and I was on my way. I discovered pretty soon that my romantic notion of watersheds wouldn't wash. The boggy bowl of the Don is often featureless and trackless, so the attractive walking route is definitely in 'enemy territory'! I saw far more of the Dearne, the Holme and the Derwent and their pleasant valleys than of the Don.

On this evening, I walked a vast panoramic landscape gaining huge views, and tracking the county boundary that followed the same logic as me. Too much of the walking was on roads, as I mistook my way, and played safe with navigation as evening and weather started to close in. At least the roads weren't busy – a teenager on a bicycle passed me four times, and I felt that strange affinity with strangers that solitude can induce. I found a pub, but it was closed; I found a bus stop, but no bus was due, so I persuaded myself my crazy plan was meant to be, and headed for my camping spot on the edge of a conifer plantation.

Once the local Friday night adventurers with their speeding cars and sound systems had disappeared, I had a quiet and cosy night among the spruce trees, sheltered from rain that never came. My Saturday route took me south, past the dramatic heather-covered slopes of Ramsden Clough, to a short pathless stretch where compass and contours saw me through. At Salter's Brook I rested by the stream in the sunshine, and then accompanied a lone cyclist up a hill for a quarter of a mile, talking a lot, until our paths divided. Later that day I met a couple, and we stopped to share stories for a few minutes, and that was it for human company for another 24 hours (although I did resort to phoning a friend!)

The route above the Derwent Valley is majestic in its wildness. When I lost the path in a detour to avoid a peat bog, my navigation became quite general. Which particular rocks I was passing I couldn't say – surely by now I must have walked another 3 miles, or was it really only one? It was clear enough by the compass and the lie of the land that I was heading the right way, and, with no pubs up here to distract my intentions, at some point I would stop, eat and sleep.

Further on, the ridges sharpened, and showed me where I was. There was a big wind rising, and it looked like it would rain quite a bit that night, so I decided I'd head down to the edge of the reservoir, and take shelter in the woods. Heading down, I took a side route that ran below the main ridge of Howden Edge, with just an inkling it may offer me a cave for shelter. Whether I had some subconscious memory of a previous discovery, or just struck lucky, I really can't say, but I found a bijou cave bedsit within a few yards!

It was a truly wild night of wind and rain, but I was well sheltered in my ideal cave. Next morning I enjoyed watching a kestrel flying past at eye level as I demolished the remainder of my food, leaving just a few snacks to get me as far as lunch back in 'civilisation'. As I walked I eked out those little treats, feeling great pleasure from each precious mouthful. There were times that morning I really deserved those snacks: during certain, possibly self-inflicted, battles survived with steep bracken-covered hillside and rushing water. Then, as I came within an hour of the road and pub, the Sunday crowds appeared in force, and I felt stranger and stranger emerging from my solitude. Aching legs took me down the last few steps to the Ladybower Inn – quite overwhelming to someone who's had a couple of days to become feral – but I managed to remember how to buy a pint and some fish and chips, and asked some strangers for a lift back to Sheffield!

I hadn't completed my project of navigating around the whole Don watershed – the Rivelin, Porter Brook and Sheaf still awaited my attention. I had experienced maybe 45 hours of solitude, in stunning landscapes, in fine weather, and felt elated and replete with it. I'd taken care of myself in the wild, connected with the essence of the place I call home, walked until I found a safe nest to sleep in – the best kind of holiday. I recommend it to you – maybe your project will be different to mine, but one day, when your chance comes, head for the hills with your home on your back!

I give here a very sketchy description of my route. There may be more elegant ways, in hindsight, and I would certainly make improvements. I hope, however, this will give you a flavour and whet your appetite.

Dearne Valley
Jenny Fortune

STAGE 1

Denby Dale station (224085) to Ellentree Brow (approx 140043)
OS Explorer Bradford and Huddersfield No. 288
Start Grid reference 224085. Length – 10 miles

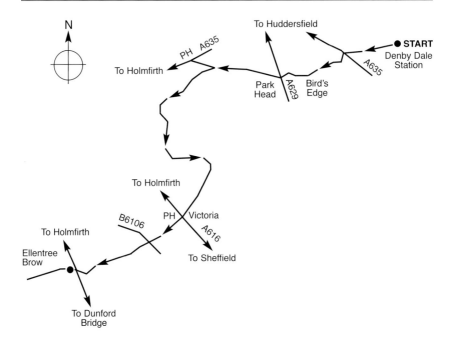

This three day walk could be made into 3 separate day walks. Finish the first day by picking up a number 20 bus, which goes near the route at Hade Edge or Harden, to Penistone for the train back to Sheffield. The second day can be finished by walking down to Kings Tree or Fairholmes for buses back to Sheffield. The Peak District Dark Peak map number OL1 covers the whole walk.

This route heads east of Denby Dale to the headwaters of the Dearne and then curves south and west around the Holme Valley.

- I took the track west from the bridge above the station, and followed the footpath/track that passes by Clay Pit, emerging on the A635 at 214084 and taking the footpath almost opposite to join the Dearne Way. You could pick up the Dearne Way from near the junction of the A635 and A636, or even from the track that goes south along the railway.

- In fact, you would be within your rights to be anywhere south of the Dearne at this point, as long as you keep north of Slack Beck and Broadstone Res, which feed into the Don. The Dearne Way is a pleasant wooded footpath along the river. At Park Head I followed the track to Piper Junction, and up through Haddingly, a route with a huge sense of space as the road climbs.

- On the brink of the great bowl that is the Holme Valley at Gate Foot (GR 183085), you can pick up the Holme Valley Circular Walk, which snakes around the valley, all the way to my camping place at Ellentree Brow. Alternatively, for majestic views, follow the road that forms the County boundary – built as it is on the watershed between the Holme and the Don/Dearne.

- There is a pub at Knowles (GR 171045), but it opens for limited hours, and there is a bus service from nearby. Taking advantage of neither, I camped in the edge of the conifer plantation, sheltered by a stone wall from local adventurers taking their sound systems for a night-time drive!

Looking back towards the Dearne from near Haddingly
Jenny Patient

Stage 2

Dark Peak OL1 Ellentree Brow (approx 140043) to Howden
Edge (approx 187940) Length – 13 miles

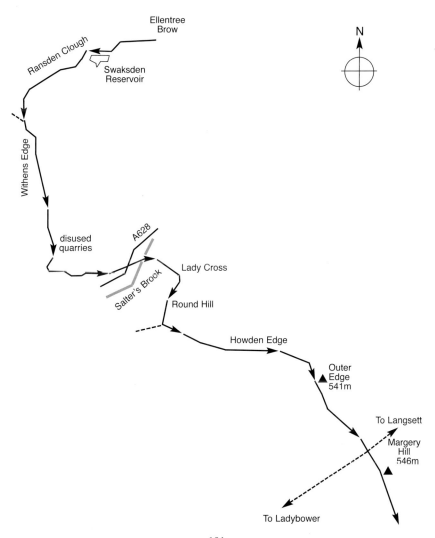

This route keeps west of Snailsden Reservoir and east of Ramsden Clough, heads south to the Transpennine Trail, then east to Lady Cross, and then follows Howden Edge in its long curve south and east.

- The track that leaves the road at GR 145041 gives a straightforward route to reach the boundary fence of Ramsden Clough, which can then be followed. From the south point of Ramsden Clough, I navigated south, until reaching the bowl of West Withens Clough, and contoured south east. Keeping broadly south, and to the contour, brings you to the disused quarries at GR 124005, with their noticeable humps and bumps. From here I followed the track that joins the TransPennine Trail, and headed east on that to where it meets the A628.

- Across this very fast road there is a beautiful spot where the old packhorse bridge crosses the Salter's Brook. Follow the track east, and at the obvious left-hand bend, take the non-obvious path straight ahead (beyond the gate), then within a few hundred metres bear right and follow the line of the old wall up the hill. As the hills tops out you'll find the Lady Cross on your right – a stone post in a carved stone base at this wonderful viewpoint. From here head roughly south west towards the summit of Round Hill and the path beyond. Go left at the path to head east and south.

- You may be able to follow this path continuously, or you may drift from it avoiding boggy bits. You can stay on track by keeping to the highest ground, with the Derwent Valley on your right and the long, soggy descent to Sheffield on your left! Your most likely error will be to descend too far towards Howden Reservoir, so keep striking out for the higher points, such as Margery Hill.

- As I approached the southern end of Howden Edge, around GR 187940, I dropped on to a lower path to the right to find a small cave that, with the wind in the right direction, made a cosy camping place. An alternative plan would be to descend to Howden dam, and camp in the woods near the reservoir, or get a lift from the car park.

Horses met near Dearne Head
Jenny Patient

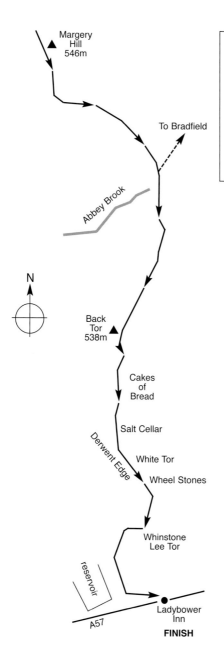

Margery Hill 546m

To Bradfield

Abbey Brook

N

Back Tor 538m

Cakes of Bread

Salt Cellar

Derwent Edge

White Tor

Wheel Stones

Whinstone Lee Tor

reservoir

A57

Ladybower Inn

FINISH

STAGE 3

Howden Edge (approx 187940) to Ladybower Inn (205865)
Length – 9 miles

The final stage heads south mostly on clear tracks, over Lost Lad and Cakes of Bread, to reach the Ladybower Inn.

- I decided on the path alongside Abbey Brook requiring steep descents through bracken, and a challenging crossing of the brook. Once on the path I headed east, and then ascended the track to the right beside Sheepfold Clough. From there each staging post was quite clear in turn, marked by well-trodden paths and peopled by bright-coloured jackets. The path that contours round the hill will take you right to the pub, without any road walking.

- From Ladybower Inn there are buses to Sheffield running to a timetable that follows no particular pattern, and plenty of scope to hitch a lift if you hit a big gap in the buses.

View of turbines from the West Yorkshire boundary road
Jenny Patient

Tips on Navigation

There are many books and courses for people interested in learning about safe navigation in the hills and countryside. It is not our purpose to give a comprehensive manual here. Having run a few navigation holidays for women, I have heard women say that they fear they cannot get to grips with navigation. They have become used to leaving the task to men. They have bought into the idea that women have little spatial awareness and cannot read maps. Courses they have been on have left them as confused and lacking in confidence as they were to begin with. This is all very depressing.

When I led a mixed party of walkers across a foggy, pathless wilderness in Scotland, safely back to our base, I heard one man say to another, "Did you think a woman could do that?" I took this as a compliment, and I hoped it meant that the man in question had learnt something and would change his opinions in future. I have also been stopped by two women on a mountain in the Lake District, asking the way because their husbands had gone ahead with the map and they were lost. The men in this case may have been able to read maps, but they lacked basic skills in party management on the hills – keep your party together and ensure everyone's safety.

When we were putting this book together some of us wanted to brush up on navigation skills, and the walk we did together to practise on is described in this book – the walk on Big Moor. We had a great deal of fun, finding ancient guide stoops and cairns, navigating across pathless heather moors, pacing out our distances. Hilariously we did manage to lose each other towards the end of the walk. It was extremely wet, much more so than normally, and a stream was almost uncrossable. I managed to get across, whilst the others walked upstream to find an alternative crossing point. After that we did not see each other again until we all met up at the vehicle. Fortunately their newly honed navigation skills stood them in good stead to find their way back, despite the growing darkness. And my attempt to find them led me into the middle of the moor where I was rewarded by the sight of a herd of red deer.

People often associate navigation with compasses, and indeed a compass is a very useful thing. But it is not something you have to use often. The most important aspects of successful navigation are to be observant and to be able to match up what is on your map with what is on the ground. The women on my courses most often said that the latter gave them the most trouble. On any map the most important thing to give you a sense of the terrain you are travelling through is the depiction of contours and features like rivers. Don't just look at footpaths, they are not always accurately drawn and may give the impression that the footpath on the ground is more visible than it actually is. Learning to read contours is fundamental.

Once with a group of women, I stopped to get them to observe a footpath that was snaking around a wooded hill. I asked them why they thought the path was winding rather than straight, and they said it was so that it could take a relatively flat course. Then the penny dropped. The winding path followed a winding contour. This may seem obvious, but it really helped them to see how the drawn contours related to real features on the ground. A good idea is to take half a large knobbly potato and cut it in slices. Draw round the base and then remove the first slice. Draw round the base and repeat. You will then have the representation of the contours of the potato drawn on your paper. A hill is like a knobbly potato, and the map consists of drawing around regular slices of it. Anything which helps you understand the representation scheme of a map will make it easier for you to follow it on a walk. Spend some time before your next walk trying to match up what you see around you with the features on the map.

Another problem can be working out which way is up and which is down. It is not always easy to see the numbers on each contour. Rivers are useful here. Rivers do tend to be at the bottom of valleys, so contours will go up from the river and towards its source. Streams will run down into it. All obvious again, but when the anxiety of doing something you have decided you are no good at kicks in, the obvious can get missed. Even an experienced walker like Nicholas Crane once described how he was looking out for a large conical hill, only to realise that the feature on the map was actually a large deep depression, not a hill at all.

Always take note of where you are on a walk regularly. If you get lost it will not be difficult to get back to a known point if you have been observing your whereabouts often. That way you should never be in the position of one man I met once on a walk, who asked me where Dungeon Gill was. When I pointed out to him that it was 8 miles away across a mountain pass, he looked visibly shaken. He had clearly come down completely the wrong side of the mountain. He wasn't even on the map that he was carrying. This should never happen if you keep alert to where you are.

Maps have various scales. In this book we have generally used 1:25,000 scale maps which means that the grid lines are spaced so that they create 1 kilometre squares. Each kilometre measures 4 centimetres on the map. Your compass should have a scale along the edge in order to measure distances fairly accurately on the map.

Navigation is fun. On Big Moor there are lots of ancient features and we set ourselves the task of travelling between some of them. This meant going off marked paths – or indeed any paths much of the time. We took compass bearings from one point to another, measured the distance and then set about finding our way.

Compass bearings can never be entirely accurate, so it is best to take them from points that are relatively near to each other, to avoid the error in the bearing amounting to a huge disparity – the further you go on a wrong bearing, the further out you will be. Once you have your bearing, the next thing is to be able to measure the distance you are travelling. There are two usual ways of doing this – pacing and timing.

Pacing requires that you have some idea how many double paces (left and right feet) you take for 100 metres. If on your map you find two clear points that are 100 metres apart you can walk between them and count your paces. I take 69. So if I need to travel 200 metres, I will count 138 paces. Equally if I am going a slightly longer distance I might work out how much time it will take me. I have an average walking speed on good terrain of about 2·5 miles per hour or 4 kilometres per hour, so a kilometre will take me 15 minutes. It is always easier to work in metres and kilometres as maps always use them.

So equipped with a bearing and timing you should be able to get from one known point to your destination. How to take a bearing is difficult to describe and better shown. I do know that many women get a bit tied up in knots trying to get their heads round it. This is not necessary.

What is a bearing? It is the number of degrees away from North that any direction is. East is 90 degrees, south 180 and west 270, there being 360 degrees in a circle.

- Place your compass on a map in line with the direction you are going to travel in

- Turn the compass housing to that the red north/south lines line up with north/south on the map; you will then have a reading on your compass of the number of degrees from north.

- There is one added complication though. The earth's magnetic north/south axis does move slightly over the years, and this of course cannot be reflected on the map. So you will have to adjust your bearing slightly to be a bit more accurate. At present if you add 3 or 4 degrees to your bearing you will be about right. So if your compass shows say 240 degrees, just add 3 or 4, to make it 243 or 244 degrees.

- Once you have your bearing, hold the compass in front of you and turn yourself around until the red needle lines up with the north south lines on the compass housing. This will then mean that just as the bearing is 243 degrees away from north, so also you are facing 243 degrees away from north. Then you can walk in the right direction.

- Pick a point to walk towards that is in that direction – preferably one that will remain visible as you walk towards it. It could be a feature on the horizon, or something much closer to hand. Or in mist a good idea if you are with others is to send someone ahead on the bearing until they are just still in view, then catch up with them. Keep repeating this.

Whenever I have taught these techniques to women there has always been a great deal of joy expressed when magically we reach the destination – the little tarn, the wall corner, the confluence of streams, whatever tiny feature it is. Of course, it isn't magic, but it feels like it. The compass work is fun, but for basic safety and the pleasure of finding your way around without having to relinquish navigation to others, get familiar with maps, contours and how features on the ground match up with what is on your map. And when you can do this you will feel so confident, you will be able to enjoy solitary walks, if that's something that interests you, and you will never again be dependent on anyone. Just imagine how lovely that will be!

SB

Useful information for women walkers

There is a huge variety of walking, cycling climbing clubs around Britain. Here are just a few of interest to women in and around Sheffield.

Red Rope – this is a socialist walking/climbing club which strives to be non-sexist, non-racist, non-elitist. Sheffield group walks fortnightly, on Sundays www.redrope.org.uk).

Hiking Dykes – Contact – Deena 0114 268 6409 or Pauline 01623 550209.

PAWW – Pooches and women who walk. This is a sociable, dog-friendly walking group in the Yorkshire area. Walks are every 4-6 weeks. Email: paww@talktalk.net

Wayward Women – Phone: Sue 0113 262 3298
Email: sue@cardinaldp.demon.co.uk

Joint Walks and Events Programme for Women in South Yorkshire

The **Women Only Walks** project has been highly successful for the past twelve years.

The initiative was set up in Rotherham in 1996 and expanded to Sheffield in January 1998 and Doncaster in 1999. New members are welcome to join. Membership is £2.00 per annum.

Our aim is to encourage women who are admittedly apprehensive or even afraid to walk alone to join in, with other like-minded women, at their own pace in a safe, friendly environment. These walks and other activities are a great opportunity to see and enjoy the local countryside or simply to get away from the domestic environment. The walks are mainly circular, usually between 4 to 10 miles. Walks are on weekdays, and weekends, and occasionally in the evenings during the summer months.

Information from the West Ranger Team on 0114 268 6196 or E-mail avril.wragg@sheffield.gov.uk

Walkingwomen Holidays
www.walkingwomen.com This is a company that specialises in women only holidays all over the UK and abroad.